Modern Persian Poetry

Modern Persian Poetry

Edited, translated and introduced by
Mahmud Kianush

The Rockingham Press

Published in 1996
by The Rockingham Press
11 Musley Lane,
Ware, Herts SG12 7EN

British Library Cataloguing-in-Publication Data

A catalogue record for this book
is available from the British Library

ISBN 1 873468 35 0

Printed in Great Britain
by Bemrose-Shafron (Printers) Ltd., Chester

Printed on Recycled Paper

CONTENTS

I dedicate this book to my dear ones:
Pari, Kaveh and Anja Kianush,
and to Jim and Katayoon Wallace.

ACKNOWLEDGEMENTS

I sincerely thank my friends Mrs. Heather Bond, Mr. Brian Bull, Miss Jill Burberry, Mr. Richard Harris and Mrs. Frances Harrison Naji, who have been the first readers of the poems of this anthology, for their valuable suggestions. I also would like to admit that there are many other contemporary Iranian poets from every one of whom I wished I could have included at least one poem in this anthology, and I hope I can find this opportunity for future editions.

M.K.

TRANSLITERATION

Although the Persian language is an Indo-European language and fundamentally different from the Arabic language, the Persian alphabet is an altered form of the Arabic which replaced the ancient Persian alphabet, Pahlavi, after the conquest of Iran by the Arabs in early seventh century. Therefore, several Arabic speech sounds or phonemes, which do not exist in Persian language, are represented by their original letters, but pronounced differently. These Arabic phonemes, which have retained their representing letters, have lost their phonemic entities to certain Persian phonemes of some similarity in pronunciation in the ears of the Persian speakers. For instance, three Arabic phonemes, "dh"(ذ), "ḍ"(ض) and "ẓ"(ظ), are pronounced as "z"(ز), which exists in both languages. In view of this obvious fact, the transliteration systems which are usually used in the West in relation to both Arabic and Persian languages, are not deemed appropriate for Persian language. Avoiding this misapprehension, the following system of transliteration, which is exclusively for Persian words, as well as Persianized Arabic words, is adopted :

CONSONANTS:

B [book]
CH [church]
D [door]
F [after]
G [good]
GH [Paris], a voiced kh, something like "r" as pronounced in French by Parisian speakers, for the Persian and Arabic (غ), as well as the Arabic (ق), for which in the universally recognized system of the transliteration for Arabic letters "q" is used.
H [house], for the Persian and Arabic "h" (ه) sound, as well as the Arabic "ḥ" (ح)
J [gem]
K [kernel]
KH [Loch], as the Scottish "ch" in the word "loch".
L [land]
M [music]

N [*news*]

P [*proper*]

R [di*r*ect]

S [*s*ound], for the Persian and Arabic "s" (س) sound, as well as Arabic "th"(ث) and "ş" (ص).

SH [fini*sh*]

T [*st*and], for the Persian and Arabic "t" (ت) sound, as well as the Arabic "ţ" (ط).

V [*v*oice], for the Persian "v" (و), as well as the Arabic "w", which is pronounced as "w" in English.

Y [*y*oung]

Z [*z*ebra], for the Persian and Arabic "z"(ز), as well as the Arabic "ẓ" (ظ), "dh" (ذ) and "ḍ" (ض).

ZH [plea*s*ure]

' [inverted apostrophe is used for the Arabic letter *ain* (ع) and the Arabic and Persian *hamza* (ء). This sound is similar to that made in English at the beginning of a word with an initial vowel.

VOWELS:

A [b*a*d, *a*dd]

E [b*e*d, sh*i*p]

EH [the French bid*et*, for the Persian words ending with this vowel]

O [*o*ld]

Â [f*a*ther]

U [f*oo*t]

I [sh*ee*p]

EY [gr*ey*]

OY [b*oy*]

OW [*ow*n]

It must be pointed out that some of the English equivalents given here for the Persian vowels are only close approximations.

INTRODUCTION

Persian poetry, whose first notable examples were written in the early ninth century AD, began to ripen in the second half of the same century with the highly artistic poems of Rudaki Samarghandi (?-950). Though of all his poems, which amounted to tens of thousands of couplets, only about eight hundred have survived, they are enough to show the excellence of his poetical imagination and his highly developed prosody:

All my teeth decayed and fell out,
Not teeth but shining lamps they were:

Beads of silver, of coral, an array of pearls,
Each one a morning star, a drop of rain ...

Gone are the days when my face was as soft as silk,
And my hair as black as tar.

Gone are the days when I was cheerful and glowing
Full of happiness, with no sorrow;

Always my fingers stroking the fragrant curls of beauties,
Always my ears to the words of men of knowledge and letters.

Gone are the days when my poems were read and praised all over the
world,
The days when I was the great poet of Khorâsân;

The days when I walked in rose gardens
Singing odes like nightingales;

The days when other poets relied on minor patrons,
But my fame and fortune came from the House of the Samanids.

Now the time has changed and I have also changed,
Bring me a walking stick and a begging sack.

Rudaki is known and praised as the father of Persian Poetry. After his death, other great poets, such as Ferdowsi, Farrokhi Sistâni, Manuchehri Dâmghâni, Anvari Abivardi, Mas'ud Sa'd Salmân, Nâser Khosrow and

Nezâmi Ganjavi, made the tenth and eleventh centuries a golden age of Persian Poetry in terms of subject matter and imagery. Their art was unique, particularly in its variety of figures of speech and musical and connotative juxtapositions. A poem could have the effect of an aural painting.

During the following three centuries, many poets emerged but most of them could not produce anything original. The bulk of their work was at the best a skilful imitation of the masters. However, in this period some great poets, like Sanâ'i Ghaznavi, Attâr Nishâburi and Jalâl od-Din Mohammad Mowlavi did produce some of the best poetical works in mysticism and Sufism. Sa'di Shirâzi's lyric and didactic poems became for many generations of poets the best examples to follow. Finally we have Shams od-Din Mohammad Hâfez (1300-1388), who undoubtedly can be regarded as the greatest critic and connoisseur of five centuries of Persian lyric poetry. He selected the most beautiful and original images of the masters for expressing his own ideas. These were more than just hackneyed illustrations of the beauty of the poet's imaginary beloved or sentimental moaning over the sorrows of separation and the burning desire for union.

Hâfez lived through a turbulent period of the history of Iran, when the regional kings or despots were continually at war with each other. They made life for the people so hard and unbearable that people found relief in fatalistic resignation. A good part of Hâfez's life was spent during the rule of Mir Mubârez od-Din, the Mozaffarid king, a cruel hypocrite who claimed to be ruling according to "shari'a" or Islamic law. He used this to deprive people of their freedom and the natural pleasures of life. Hâfez, infusing his images with double and sometimes triple meanings, wrote poems that can be taken as either love poems mixed with praise for the kings and other authorities, or mystical poems mixed with philosophical ideas. He also cleverly expressed remarks about the political and social situation of the nation.

> Life with a single moment of sorrow
> is not worth the whole world:
> Sell our ragged garment of piety for some wine,
> no better thing you can get for it.

> How priceless is the prayer-mat of piety,
> they do not accept it
> For a cup of wine in the street of wine-sellers!

The pomp of a king's crown,
   in which lies the fear of life,
Is a heart-alluring head-dress,
   but not worth losing one's head.

Like Hâfez put your heart in contentment
   and turn away from the mean world
For taking one grain of favour from the miserly
   is not worth a mountain of gold.

Hâfez's achievement was an artistic miracle, yet he was not able to give a new direction to Persian poetry. After him until the appearance of the Safavids in the fifteenth century, Persian poetry followed the paths paved by the great poets of the past, without any fundamental changes in form and subject matter. The Safavids, who brought about a marriage between the government and the clergy and declared Shi'ism as the official religion, were not good patrons for poets and musicians. Poets were encouraged to write religious poems, eulogies and elegies for the Shi'ite saints and martyrs. But few poets sacrificed their art for securing royal patronage, and many of them turned to other occupations for their livelihoods. Consequently they lost the incentive for creating art of a high standard. Some poets emigrated to India where the Moghul kings, who liked to imitate the pre-Safavid Persian royal customs, enthusiastically received and encouraged them.

Edward G. Brown, the famous British Iranologist, said: "One of the most curious and, at first sight, inexplicable phenomena of the Safawi period is the extraordinary dearth of notable poets in Persia during the two centuries of its duration. Architecture, miniature-painting and other arts flourished exceedingly; the public buildings with which Shah Abbas adorned his realms, and especially his capital Isfahan, have not ceased to command the admiration of all who beheld them from his time until the present day ... Yet, though poets innumerable are mentioned in the Tuhfa-i Sami and other contemporary biographies and histories, there is hardly one ... worthy to be placed in the first class. During the seventy stormy years of Timur's life there were at least eight or ten poets besides the great Hafiz, who outshone them all, whose names no writer on Persian literature could ignore; while during the two hundred and twenty years of Safawi rule there was in Persia, so far as I have been able to ascertain, hardly one of conspicuous merit or originality. I say 'in Persia' advisedly, for a brilliant group of poets from Persia, of whom Urfi of Shirâz (d. A.D.1590) and Sa'eb of Isfahan (d. A.D.1670) are perhaps the most notable, adorned the court of the 'Great Moghuls' in India, and these

11

were in many cases not settlers or the sons of emigrants, but men who went from Persia to India to make their fortunes and returned home when their fortunes were made. This shows that it was not so much lack of talent as lack of patronage which makes the list of distinctively Safawi poets so meagre." (*Literary History of Persia*, vol. IV, pp. 24-27)

The Safavids' disapproval of worldly poetry had one good outcome which was the separation of the poets from the court and the emergence of poetry as an independent popular art. Poets broke away from describing luxurious, majestic scenes of life as could be seen in the royal court and began to observe ordinary people with all their daily problems, hopes, desires and sorrows. This led to a fundamental change in poetic vision and sources of imagery. Poets became something of a mouthpiece for the silent, simple people, reflecting their sufferings and aspirations in their works. They addressed an abstract tyrant in terms of World, Time and The Hand of Fate.

In this period a style of poetry, which was not completely new, was pursued by many poets. Its main feature was an emphasis on the use of metaphors in every line, most of them obscure and enigmatic. These poets were also very fond of using didactic couplets in their lyrical poems (ghazals), giving them the air of proverbs, or simply incorporating into them the well known proverbs. Sâ'eb Tabrizi (1607-1675), the most distinguished among these poets, proudly called the style "strange", meaning not as familiar to people as the traditional styles of poetry. Later this style was known as "Indian Style" because it was put to great use by many of those Iranian poets who had migrated to India. It was also referred to as "Esfahâni" style, because Sâ'eb and many of his followers lived in Esfahân or Isfahan.

Sâ'ib, do not ask me to return home,
What first caused my separation from home were my "strange"
thoughts...

So "strange" has become my imagery, Sâ'eb,
That I do not expect anyone's appreciation.

These poems were understood and appreciated by few and only a relatively small number of the simpler didactic lines from their ghazals were adopted by people, and sometimes used by them in conversation or writing.

Towards the early eighteenth century, by the time of the Ghâjârids, Persian poetry had atrophied. Some poets turned away, not only from the Indian but also other styles which had been followed since the fifteenth century. A number of poets returned to the style of the eleventh century masters such as Manuchehri, Onsori, Farrokhi, Mas'ud Sa'd Salmân and Anvari, as a means of halting the decline. The most successful among the pioneers of this movement was Ghâ'âni Shirâzi (1807-1853), but he, like his masters, was a court poet and most of his poems were panegyrics. He was not in touch with the social changes which were soon to lead to the Constitutional Revolution in Iran (1905).

With the emergence of newspapers in Iran, which opened the way for political and literary magazines, change in the written and literary language was one of the essential elements of any movement towards the modernization of literature in general. All the writers and poets who were looked upon as torchbearers of progress, with all the differences in their ideological and political views, agreed on one thing: the necessity for change as a prerequisite for progress. But when they came to explain what they meant by or expected from change, they basically differed in their arguments. Their debates, which were carried in newspapers and literary periodicals, clearly showed that there were two opposing groups — one believing that progress, as with changes in all aspects of social life, including literature, could not be achieved without a radical departure from the past, while the other insisted, at least, on the preservation of the traditional rules of prosody and aesthetic niceties which, they believed, reached perfection with the great poets of the eleventh to fifteenth centuries, such as Ferdowsi, Nezâmi, Sa'di and Hâfez.

In one particularly historic debate, the writer and editor of the magazine *Tajaddod* (Renaissance), Taghi Raf'at, who was himself a poet and through his knowledge of French and Turkish languages familiar with modern thought and literature in Europe, wrote a series of essays in 1918, in support of another writer who had been furiously attacked by the "conservative" side. The reason for their criticism was an article, published under the title "The School of Sa'di", in a newspaper called *Zabân-e Âzâd* (Free Speech), in which the writer boldly had expressed his revolutionary opinions. Taghi Raf'at seized the opportunity to give voice to some of the essential views of the "Progressive" side of the debates. He wrote:

"The writer of the article "The School of Sa'di" deserves to be appreciated and admired ... Such a rebellion was necessary; the political revolution of Iran needed such a complementary venture. The uprising required an initial move. The writer of the article published in *Zabân-e Âzâd* gave the starting signal, and now young intellectuals can, and should, attack the fortress of despotism and conservatism in literature, because we ought to be children of our time. The sounds of rifles and guns rising from the international

13

battlefields [World War I] create in us nervous tensions, which cannot be tranquillized or interpreted by the old, smooth musical and static language Sa'adi and, relatively speaking, his contemporaries used in their poems, or in fact in their litanies. We have needs which the people of Sa'di's time did not. We are affected by adverse national and political currents which we cannot expect Sa'di to have ever imagined. We find in ourselves and in our environment material and spiritual deficiencies, not one of which Sa'di has touched upon; and finally, we are living in an age when even 13-year old school children are much more knowledgeable in different branches of science and technology ... In view of these facts, we expect you, at present, not to talk to us, the disturbed and apprehensive youth of this age of awakening, about Sa'di, Hâfez and Ferdowsi. Instead, explain to us the meaning of life. Show us the way to success and salvation. Give wings to our spirits, and power and glory to our minds ... Drive away the nightmares of decline and collapse from before our eyes ... In our view, this [modernization of literature] is not exclusively a literary problem, but also a combination of various social and national problems, and therefore, it is essentially important. The literature of every nation is a mirror in which the features of that nation's culture and civilization are reflected ... Moreover, we always bear in mind an opinion expressed by Victor Hugo, the French Romantic poet; an opinion that is obviously relevant to the history of the present nations. He said: "The most decisive direct result of a political revolution is a literary revolution; do not involve yourselves in material evolutions, unless with an intellectual revolution." (Yahyâ Ariyanpur, *From Sabâ to Nimâ* (Tehran, 1961) vol. II, pp.436-453)

In another article, which was something of a manifesto of the revolutionary liberals and published in a short-lived magazine called *Âzâdestân* (Freedomland), Taghi Raf'at said: "Language is a means for the expression of man's thoughts and emotions. If it could be claimed and proved that the thoughts and sentiments of mankind have never undergone any changes throughout history, then it would have been reasonably argued that language might also remain in a perpetually stable state with no need for any changes ... It is an obvious fact that any intellectual and material reform necessitates a reform in literature ... because to us it is impossible to think that something can be changed in essence without being changed in form ..." (*From Sabâ to Nimâ*, vol. II, p.463)

The essential purpose of the new poetry, for both the traditionalists and the radical progressives, was the expression of political, social and patriotic ideas; criticizing the politicians and statesmen for their reactionary ideas and unjust practices; awakening the people by explaining to them the hopeless state of affairs of the nation, and by enlightening them about their rights and their deprivations; and bringing them new, progressive thought from the developed, modern world, so that they could have some credible basis for a comparative evaluation of their own traditional beliefs and concepts. But the traditionalists insisted that all this could be successfully done in the forms and styles inherited from the great poets of the past, who did not see any need to change them for about a thousand years. Even one of the most famous poets among the Traditionalists, Malek-osh-Sho'arâ Bahâr, who was highly praised and respected for his masterly research in Persian language and literature, in reaction to the writer of the article "The School of Sa'di", said authoritatively: "I claim that every principle and rule (in poetry) can be found in Sa'di's Bustân and Hâfez's ghazals."

However, when we consider the practice of these two opposing groups by reading their poems, we find that the Traditionalists have not deviated from the old forms and have kept their diction as close as possible to that of the great masters, while the Progressives in some of their poems have brought about some changes in the arrangements of rhymes to produce new forms but, like the Traditionalists, have used the same old metres. It is only the language of the Progressives which is different, being simpler and to some extent closer to common speech and, therefore, more appealing to the common people. They also took less care in the artistic structure of their poems, which for the Traditionalists was very important. A few lines from a gasideh by Malek-osh-Sho'arâ Bahâr, entitled "A Critical Tribute to Sir Edward Grey" (translated by Edward Brown in his book, "The Press and Poetry of Modern Persia: Specimens of The Political and Patriotic Poetry of Modern Persia") is a good example of the style, form and diction in the poetry produced by the Traditionalists:

> To London speed, O Breeze of dawning day,
> Bear this my message to Sir Edward Grey.
> To thee in skill, wise Councillor of State,
> Ne'er did the world produce a peer or mate! ...
> "When fortune frowns on man," the proverb goes,
> "His wisest act no good resultant shows."
> Alas that thou, for all thy wits, has wrought
> A deed which save regret can yield thee naught!
> For India's gates, closed for a hundred years,
> To Russia now you open without fears.
> You nurse the wolf-cub in your arm: a deed
> Which folly prompts, and which to grief will lead.
> To this o'erbearing partner you submit,

And bow your head, bereft of sense and wit.
Your pacts with Russia made in time gone by
Brought loss unseen by your short-sighted eye ...

Its poetical expression aside, the subject of the above poem is a political event which could have regrettable national and international consequences. This can be compared to a poem about a topic of more immediate concern to the common people, the making of a corner in wheat or bread at a time when there was an economic crisis, and this too can be considered to have a political nature. A progressivist, Mirzâ Hosayn Tabibzâdeh, poetically surnamed "Kamâl", wrote a short poem in which he attacked the wheat-cornerers. A comparison between his poem and Malek-osh-Sho'arâ's ghasideh, clearly shows that the conflict between the Traditionalists and Progressives about the scope for the modernization of poetry was related to form and style rather than to subject matter and the poetical outlook:

So long as the fingers of the bread-cornerers are on the bread
There is unrest in the world and ruin in the age.
That fair ascendant star of Justice is eclipsed;
That beauteous face of Equality is hidden.
O hungry child, cry not thus, or else
There will be a slap on the face from the hands of the bread-cornerers!
O mother, surrender that ornament of thy embrace to the earth,
For a human life is cheaper than a mouthful of bread!
The pen is wearied of talking so much of bread;
The pages of "Kamâl" are dyed with blood: what hurt is there in this?

The Traditionalists themselves had their own differences and may be divided into different groups. There were those who imitated the classical poets virtually in everything and produced some poor, lifeless imitations, which were either read in their own isolated poetry societies or published in a few not-so popular periodicals. There were those who, like Malek-osh-Sho'arâ Bahâr, had deep knowledge and understanding of Persian classical poetry and tried not to imitate but to revive the styles of the great masters, while expressing their own ideas and emotions. These could be known as the Neo-classicists or as they are called by many critics, the Revivalists. Finally, there were those who did not limit their experiments to certain styles and forms, but let their varied subject matter direct them in choosing and altering the traditional styles and forms, mainly relying on their own tastes for their diction. Among the best-known of these poets is Âref Ghazvini, (1882-1933) who owes his success and fame more to his political and patriotic songs (Tasnif), than to his ghazals and other forms of poetry. Another such poet is Mirzâdeh Eshghi (1893-1923), a revolutionary poet of extremist ideas, whose best achievements are his dramatic and long narrative poems. One of these poems is "Eshghi's Ideal, in Three Scenes", in which the poet relates the tragic life of a patriotic man, whose two sons are killed in the fighting during the Constitutional Revolution of Iran, leading to the death of his wife from grief. His only daughter, Maryam, having been seduced and led to a wretched and unchaste life by the debauched son of an aristocrat family, commits suicide. Both of these dramatic poems were remarkably new in their themes and the style of expression, but not in their forms and rhyme patterns.

Iraj Mirzâ Jalâl-ol-Molk (1874-1925) is another prominent figure of this third group of the Traditionalists, himself one of the Ghâjâr princes, with a good knowledge of the French language. But being a rather enlightened intellectual of his time, he found himself particularly at home employing his poetic power and skill in versification when he wrote narrative poems in couplet form (masnavi). His style of language was close to common speech in its lucidity and idiomatic fluency, and rich with vivid colloquial expressions. Through these poems he attacked the hypocritical conduct of the clergy, superstitious beliefs, religious restrictions, women's social deprivations and many ideas and traditions which could be considered as the indication of national backwardness. His satirical tone sometimes let his witticism enter the domain of ribald humour and was so amusing and pungent in its expressiveness that many of his lines spread from mouth to mouth, giving them a proverbial and anecdotal quality. In his "Âref-nâme" — a long poem of more than five hundred couplets, addressed to Âref Ghazvini — he deals with the matter of hejâb and the chador (or Islamic veil for women) and relates a story about a woman in a chador who can easily surrender to the pleasure of sex with a stranger but, being zealous in observing the religious law, succeeds in keeping her head and face covered with her chador throughout lovemaking, so as not to be seen by the man. Then Iraj talks about the real chastity of women for which wearing a chador cannot be the sign of existence, and says:

Beautiful is created your face
For the delight of our eyes.
Women are flowers in the garden of life;
They are roses and jasmines.
Would the grace of a rose's face be blemished
If the poor nightingale cast a glance at it?
It wouldn't do any harm to a flower
If a butterfly rested on its petals a while.

In general, the most outstanding feature of the poetry of this period, which indicated a clear departure from the past, was the new role of poetry in the intellectual and political life of the people. The courts of kings, the guest halls of statesmen and aristocrats and the book-shelves in the homes of those few who could afford to commission calligraphers for producing copies of the works of their favourite poets, now had been replaced by the pages of newspapers and magazines, where the poems were companions to news and political articles and social debates. Thus poetry had to come down from its purely artistic throne to express the political emotions and social aspirations of the ordinary people, the readers of the press. This new function, with its narrow scope, for some time satisfied many poets, with some insignificant changes in form and style, as well as in diction. But for a number of poets, who wanted a real revolution in Persian poetry, this was not enough to be accepted as Modernism. For these poets, who were well aware of all the shackles of traditional prosody, it was only the beginning of efforts to explore and experiment with the modernization of Persian poetry. For a thousand years "form" had been, directly or indirectly, the key to the composition of Persian poetry. However, the modernizers sought to use poetry in their fight against injustice by versifying political ideas and social insights. To do this meant incorporating a number of modern and colloquial words, hitherto considered "unpoetical", and thus narrowing the wide gap between poetic idiom and everyday Persian. Such liberated attitudes were indirect opposition to the shackles of the formalist tradition.

Here we must look back at the traditional forms of Persian poetry. From the beginning of the Islamic era, when poets such as Hanzaleh Bâdghisi (early ninth century A.D.) wrote the first poems in an evolved Persian language called "Fârsi-ye Dari", their model was an Arabic form called the "ghasideh" (qasida). The ghasideh is a type of ode with a single rhyme, extending from 15 to 100 or even more distiches or couplets. In the course of time, several other forms were developed, each suitable for certain themes. Of these forms the most widely used were:

1　Ghazal, which bears some similarity to the "sonnet" in subject matter and, like the ghasideh, is in mono-rhyme, but runs from 4 to 14 distiches, incorporating the pen name of the poet in the final couplet.

2　Masnavi, or rhyming couplet, used for heroic and romantic, as well as didactic, compositions.

3　Rubâ'i, or quatrain, in an unvarying metre, mostly used for philosophical, mystical and lyrical themes. The best quatrains (rubâ'iyât) ever written are those of Omar Khayyam of Nishabur (d.1123).

In all these forms, particularly in the ghasideh and ghazal, rhyme always had a great influence on the formation of a poet's ideas. Sometimes the rhyme would act as a " muse" for poets, leading through association to ideas for further lines. Only a few poets had the ability to dominate the form and rhyme with their poetical creativity and remain relatively free from the limitations of classical prosody. As a result, poets copied old motifs, just as Persian carpet weavers do for their patterns.

Among the poets who continued their experiments towards a radical modernization of Persian poetry, it was Nimâ Yushij (1896-1959) who took revolutionary measures to establish a new perspective in Persian poetry. He began writing poetry when he was a high school student, and the person who encouraged him by reading his poems and helping him to improve his versification, was one of his teachers, Nezâm Vafâ (1883-1960), himself a lyric poet who wrote simple love poems in the classical style, mingled with pieces of romantic poetical prose. Until the age of twelve Nimâ Yushij had lived in Yush, a village in the northern province of Mâzandarân, near the Caspian Sea, where his father was a farmer. In his speech to the First Congress of Iranian Writers, 1946, in Tehran, Nimâ Yushij said: "My first years of life were spent among the shepherds and horse-herders who, in their seasonal movements from one grassland to another, every evening sat round the fire on the mountainside for long hours. From my childhood years I remember nothing but savage fights, and other things related to a nomadic life, and the simple amusements of those people in an atmosphere of monotony and ignorance. I learned reading and writing from the Âkhund [preacher and teacher] of the village where I was born. He used to run after me through the alleyways and, catching me, tied my thin feet to rough, thorny trees and beat me with long canes. He had made a scroll by pasting together some letters which peasants had written to their relatives, and he ordered me to learn the whole scroll by heart."

From his father, a boastful man, skilled in horse riding, hunting and playing the tar (Persian lute), Nimâ Yushij inherited a naive but strong sense of pride which could be interpreted as arrogance. His mother, mild in nature, born and bred in a family of good education and learning, knew by heart many classical stories, such as Nezâmi's " Haft Peykar " (The Seven Beauties), and many poems, specially Hâfez's ghazals, which she related and recited to him. This was how Nimâ became so fascinated with Nezâmi and Hâfez and remained an ardent admirer of their work all his life. In the long years of experimenting with different forms of classical poetry, he tried to imitate Nezâmi by writing a dramatic long poem, about 1500 couplets, and the result is "Ghal'e-ye Seghrim" (Seghrim Fortress), the most unskilful work of its kind ever written in Persian, displaying all the shortcoming of a novice in composition and versification; so unsmoothed and jumbled in its phraseology that it has become almost unreadable. He also tried to imitate Hâfez in writing ghazals. He was so unsuccessful that he stopped the experiment after composing a few ghazals which came out as ridiculous parodies. His attempts in imitating Abd-dor-Rahmân Jâmi (1414-1492) and Jalâl-od-Din Rumi in writing didactic anecdotes in verse, and Omar Khayyam in composing rubâ'is (quatrains), did not go beyond the level of crude exercises. Out of his six hundred or so rubâ'is, there is only one which is usually quoted as his own impression about his innovative measures in the modernization of Persian poetry and releasing it from the classical prosody:

> With my poetry I have driven the people into a great conflict;
> Good and bad, they have fallen in confusion;
> I myself am sitting in a corner, watching them:
> I have flooded the nest of ants.

Nimâ Yushij continued these experiments until 1937, when he wrote his first symbolist free verse, "The Phoenix", in which he successfully employed what he had learned from some of the French symbolists. Until then his dependence on classical forms had not allowed him to enter a completely new realm of poetry. The only exception was a long lyric poem in a dramatic style, " Fantasy" (Afsâneh) which he had written about fifteen years before "The Phoenix". This poem which, even today, some critics consider as his masterpiece, is not quite new in form. It is in one of the less used classical metres with equal lines throughout the poem, in five-line stanzas, rhymed in the second and fourth lines. But its subject, a romantic dialogue between a "lover" and "Fantasy", in which the poet has expressed his emotional experience of love, and his idealistic interpretation of life, was at the time of its publication (1921) new enough in Persian poetry to be considered "Modern". Manifest in " Fantasy" is a mixture of Hâfez's mystical lyricism, Nezâmi's dramatic observation of life, Khayyam's half epicurean, half-fatalistic world view, the French Romantics' preoccupation with self and social justice, and the Symbolists' suggestive expression through metaphors and symbols. All this is reflected in the mirror of simple, clear language, and could have remained as the most fitting poetic persona for Nimâ Yushij; but his ambition to give Persian poetry a completely new identity, took him too far in learning lessons from some of the French Symbolists, especially the Belgian Emile Verhaeren (1855-1916). Verhaeren had declared: "The old are obedient to general laws of prosody and grammar, while the latter [the young Belgian Symbolists] seek their form in themselves, forging their own order and submitting only to individual rules which spring from their own way of thinking and feeling". His vocabulary bristled with colloquialisms, and in many cases he used nouns as adjectives and adverbs as substantives. His critics said that he cultivated his faults; they accused him of being ignorant of the French language pointing out that grammar and syntax were objects of his derision. Some of the outstanding characteristics of his poetry were the repetition of the first statement throughout the theme of a poem; using rhyme only when and where he felt it would accentuate the rhythm; and his attention to the "gloomier aspects of nature" and, in several of his books, the incessant use in titles of the word *soir* (night).

While these were all natural and individual characteristics of Verhaeren in his poetry, they were adopted by Nimâ Yushij as his principles in modernizing his poetry. Nimâ's native language was Tabari, one of the many Persian dialects, which are spoken but not written in different provinces. This he deliberately let have its effect in the standard Persian language of his poetry. He made a constant virtue in his poetic art of his weakness in versification, which dislocated and confused the order of words to the extent of unnecessary ambiguities. He searched Persian classical poetry for words which are now obsolete and used them along with some colloquial words. Using local names for birds, trees, flowers, and many other things was for him a way of enriching the texture of his diction. He even zealously avoided using many adverbs and compound verbs as they were.

One of the deepest factors of Verhaeren's influence on Nimâ Yushij, was in the realm of subject matter. Nimâ, like him employed the image of night in most of his modern poems; but for Nimâ Yushij, who lived in a time when a new dictatorship was established in Iran by Rezâ Shah, the founder of the Pahlavi dynasty, "night" became the symbol of the dark situation of society, of tyranny and injustice, of poverty and ignorance, and of everything that people wanted to be ended. In contrast to "night", were "morning", "dawn", "day" and their herald, "the cock" and its "crow", by which the people who are in sleep of a wretched life might be awakened to welcome the light of freedom and enlightenment. Soon the idea of Nimâ Yushij's "night" and "morning" were taken up by many of the younger poets with the same symbolic meanings, and expanded with new symbols, such as "tomorrow" (the day of uprising and freedom), "the army of the night" (the government and its army and police), "the vigilant of the night" (the active opposition forces), or "nightingale" and "lark" (those intellectuals who do not remain silent), etc.

What made Nimâ Yushij a great, powerful guru for the young poets of his time were his innovations in form and style rather than the content of his poetry. He came to the scene of change at a time when all the conservative efforts of the Neo-classicists, Revivalists and others had failed to free Persian poetry from the long decadence which was, to a great extent, the result of the ruling power of prosody over subject matter. The quantitative metres in Persian verse are numerous and they have equal possibilities for being broken and used in making lines of different lengths in a poem; but classical forms did not allow this. The other great obstacle to any innovation in the rhythmic construction of poems, was the fixed pattern of rhymes in different forms. Moreover, the unit for sentences in verse was the " beyt", two equal lines rhymed as their forms permitted. Therefore, a complete thought, the content of a sentence, had to be expressed in the confines of one beyt. In other words, the beyt was the actual stanza in any form of poetry. It was only free verse that could break all these fetters of Persian prosody, and it was Nimâ Yushij who, by using his knowledge of the *vers libre* of the French Symbolists, specially in Emile Verhaeren poems, and adapting it to the Persian poetic language, accomplished this revolutionary work. Lines became the phrases and sentences, and beyts (or stanzas) became the paragraphs of a poem, and the pattern of rhymes in each paragraph of a poem was especially decided and arranged for that paragraph by the poet. Using all these possibilities resulted not only in freedom in form, but also gave a new perspective to Persian poetry. Now a poem, for instance a ghazal, was not to be composed of a number of unrelated, or rather incoherent, thoughts or ideas, connected together by the fixed pattern of rhymes in the equal lines of a certain form. In Nimâ-esque modern prosody, the subject of a poem attained its right continuity and integrity, as well as the coherence it needed for its parts. Thus one poem, as its subject required, could be completed in only a few lines, and another in pages of lines and paragraphs of different lengths. In this way Persian Poetry, while maintaining its own independence, gained after a thousand years the unbounded freedom of prose. This was the real achievement of Nimâ Yushij and the reason for his being acclaimed as the founder, or the father, of modern Persian poetry.

As time passed, Nimâ Yushij became more and more obsessed with form and style in his poetry, and his themes became less and less varied. In fact, he began to repeat himself, especially with social and political motifs, and wrote many poems which were devoid of his earlier typical romantic lyricism, though still rich with vivid descriptions of nature. Fortunately, the qualities of spontaneity and lucidity remained alive in nearly all the short poems he wrote in his native dialect, Tabari. Of all his poems written when his modern style developed to perfection, only a few, such as "O, People!", " My Heart of Steel" and "The Amen Bird" (Morgh-e Âmmin) have been as much widely read, appreciated and printed in anthologies, as " Fantasy".

Among the first young poets who became excited by Nimâ Yushij's innovations in form, style and poetic perspective, was Fereydun Tavallali (1919-1985), an archaeologist by profession, from Shirâz. He had made a name for himself by writing satirical parodies in rhymed prose intermingled with verse, following mainly Sa'di's "Golestân" (Rose Garden). Tavallali was much more experienced in Persian traditional prosody than Nimâ Yushij, and therefore, his poetic outlook was developed by the influence of the classical, specially lyric, poetry. Nevertheless, as a progressive intellectual, Tavallali was motivated enough by the idea of modernization in all aspects of life to fall under the spell of Nimâ Yushij's revolutionary experiments in form, so much so that he went from his home town, Shirâz, to Tehran to see him. His faithfulness however to the prosodic principles of classical poetry, with which his poetic skill was moulded, was so strong that soon he found himself disillusioned with the Master, especially when Nimâ Yushij took steps to change the aesthetic norms of poetry far beyond the grasp of disciples like himself. In an introduction to his second book, "Musk Bag" (Nâfeh, 1962), Tavallali attacked those followers of Nimâ Yushij whom he categorized as "Nonsense-talkers", and said:

"In fact, it was a long time since Nimâ himself had given up the form and style he had introduced in his " Fantasy", and instead, by writing poems, the unequal lines of which were full of ambiguities, he thought that, with this "tangled hank", he had accomplished his mission in revolutionization of poetry."

Tavallali's classical and romantic understanding of poetic perspective did not allow him to advance in modernization beyond a few changes in form. He wrote poems in stanzas of four equal lines, in some poems the fourth line is shorter than the others. This form was, and still is, so widely used by many poets, specially the followers of Tavallali, that by some critics the name of the form was given to a group of poets, and they are called "Four-liners" (Chahâr-pâreh Sorâyân). Tavallali was deeply influenced by the lyric poets of the past. In fact most of his poems are either expansions of the themes of a single "beyt" (distich) of classical ghazals, or a whole ghazal with a new rhyming pattern. Some of his best poems are those written in a descriptive, in some cases a narrative, form, recounting his personal moods and feelings, or of his beloved's behaviour. In his subject matter he is sentimental and he expresses his feelings with romantic exaggeration, in a very flowery language, full of decorative and musical imagery.

The political situation of Iran, specially after the Shah's *coup d'état* in 1953, and the overthrow of the nationalist government of Mosaddeq, created an atmosphere of despair and pessimism among the Iranian intelligentsia. Many of the writers, poets and artists turned to narcotics to make the frustrating shock of defeat bearable to themselves. This remedy went, of course, hand in hand with fatalism, defeatism and escapism, which were beautifully expressed by poets like Tavallali. Another, equally strong, tranquilliser was erotic pleasure in poetry and fiction. And that was how a poet like Tavallali, who, before the *coup d'état*, was full of hope, and to some extent revolutionary, in his poetic vision, allowed pessimism and eroticism to become the most essential themes in his poetry. His first book, "The Unchained" (Rahâ), published in 1950, begins with a rousing poem entitled "The Tomorrow of Revolution". The majority of the poems in his second book, "The Musk Bag" (Nâfeh, an allusion to its content as being a mixture of the poet's artistic power and the essence of his sorrows) have very melancholic, depressing themes, of which "The Disgrace of Lingering" is an example:

> What is the meaning of being a plaything
> > in the hands of futility?
> To be contaminated with the sin of fathers!
> To bear this heavy yoke of life,
> Submitted to weariness and decay!
> Life is like a road and we are wayfarers;
> How long can we tread the over-trodden paths?
> To be under this blue firmament
> Is not worth the fear of not to be.
> Do not ask the mill about the grains;
> One is the crusher and the other the crushed.
> The world is everlasting for itself,
> Though in a perpetual ebb and flow;
> It is you and I who must leave
> Our offspring behind and disappear.
> I am terribly ashamed of the disgrace of lingering;
> How blessed it is to die and to be relieved.

Tavallali, with his deep knowledge of the classical technique of prosody, could write highly wrought poems, elegant in their well-chosen words which

24

were in harmony with his romantic lyricism. His innovations firmly bound to Persian traditional form and diction, could be easily appreciated and followed by the majority of young poets, whom he called the "True Modernists" and he said of them: "These poets have made it their duty to study and acquire thorough knowledge of the works and thoughts of our classics, and to venerate the glorious masters of our traditional poetry; and though, in view of the fact that Persian poetry calls for right and proper change, they are in search of new principles and rules, and always believe that there is no doubt their efforts would never produce any desirable result, if they were not based on the traditional heritage and criteria."

Thus the movement towards the modernization of Persian poetry took two different directions: one led by Tavallali, and the other by Nimâ Yushij himself. For those who followed Tavallali, the horizons of how poetry could develop were opened up by the great masters of a literary heritage over a thousand years old. No matter what their social concerns and ideological beliefs were, in their attitude towards poetry they were conditioned by classical principles and values. They lived in a new age, they had a new understanding of life and the universe, but they let their feelings and emotions be shaped by traditional inspiration and aestheticism. In their expressions of the new ideals of modern man one could often hear the tone of the old masters. A Marxist who advocated the necessity of a socialist revolution might have the same patterns of thought as those of an idealist bourgeois, who could not accept any changes beyond some democratic reforms. In the domain of the modernist movement where Tavallali was the most influential figure, there were poets with every type of individual disposition and social inclinations. Yet, many of these poets thought of themselves as the followers of Nimâ Yushij, only because it was Nimâ Yushij who had been known as the true founder of modern poetry, or free verse, and not Tavallali. Among them were poets who would establish themselves after a few years, such as Fereydun Moshiri, Siyâvash Kasrâ'i, Mohammad Zohari, Hassan Honarmandi, Hushang Ebtehâj ("H.E. Sâyeh"), and Nâder Nâderpur, and about a decade later of a younger generation, Manuchehr Âtashi, Mahmud Mosharraf Âzâd Tehrâni ("M. Âzâd"), Forugh Farrokhzâd (with her three books before the publication of "Born Again", in which her poetry was completely changed in style and diction) and Mohammad Rezâ Shafi'i Kadkani.

Surprisingly, the true followers of Nimâ Yushij were those poets who did not follow him by adopting his strange syntactic changes in language and his other peculiar innovations, but like him searched for new forms and styles so that they could make their own experiments and find their own way towards modernity. The most prominent among this group of poets were Ahmad

Shâmlu ("A. Bâmdâd"), Nosrat Rahmâni, Bijan Jalâli, Sohrâb Sepehri, Mehdi Akhavân Sâless ("M. Omid") and of a younger generation, Yadollâh Royâ'i, Forugh Farrokhzâd (after freeing herself from the influence of Tavallali), Mahmud Kiânush, Esmâ'il Kho'i and Ahmad Rezâ Ahmadi.

Ahmad Shâmlu was only fourteen years of age when the Second World War broke out. Towards the end of the war, when Iran was occupied by the allies, he began writing poetical pieces in prose. His themes were love, nature and a nationalistic patriotism, which was an emotional reaction to the invasion of his country. After the war, when the Communist Party of Iran (Tudeh Party) established itself as the most progressive social force, many of the young writers and poets either joined it or became, like Ahmad Shâmlu, its sympathizers. By this time Ahmad Shâmlu, who had some knowledge of Persian prosody and could now stand above his juvenilia, "The Forgotten Songs" (Âhanghâ-ye Farâmush Shodeh) turned to Nimâ Yushij and for some time imitated him in style and even poetic diction. But unlike Nimâ Yushij, who was rather obsessed with form and style, Shâmlu was diligently in his quest for modern themes and this was a realm in which Nimâ Yushij could not offer a rich source of inspiration. To Shâmlu poetry was recognizable only when it could stand naked, stripped of all artistic ornaments and still shine with clear imaginative beauty. This attitude was formed by two fundamental factors in the course of his initial experiences in the art of poetry. The first was the formative effect of writing poems in prose, and the second his acquaintance with European, especially French poetry and the poetry of other nations through French or Persian translations. In this way he began his journey in the world of the foreign poets and among them he became fascinated with Paul Eluard, Louis Aragon, Federico Garcia Lorca, Vladimir Mayakovsky and Nâzim Hikmet, the famous Turkish poet. In the works of each of these poets he found something in agreement with his poetic nature. Like Eluard, Shâmlu addresses women as those "whose love is life itself" and "whose wrath is death", and greets them with these words:

> You who have illuminated the despair of heavens
> With the hope of stars;
> You who have created years
> And centuries;
> And have given birth to men who have engraved their mottos
> On the gallows;
> And have nurtured the great history of the future with hope
> In your small wombs ..."
> *(The Fresh Air).*

And again like Eluard, for whom "woman becomes a kind of mirror ... in which the motions of the universe are reflected" (The Twentieth-century Criticism, Vol. 7, p. 243), Shâmlu became so fascinated with this metaphor that not only has he used it in many of his poems, but he has put it in the titles of two of his books, "The Garden of Mirror" and "Âydâ in the Mirror", Âydâ being his third wife.   In this way, everything has been a free source of inspiration for Shâmlu, but whatever he had created bears his own mark. Through his wonderful ability of absorbing the inspiring ideas, thoughts and images in the works of any poet and writer, he opened the frontiers of World Poetry to the eyes of the young poets who, before him, were confined to the scope of the traditional poetic vision.

Shâmlu's style reached the peak of perfection when he completely abandoned rhythm and rhyme, and gave to his work the natural music of the Persian language, using soft and harmonious words to make his poems different from ordinary prose.   It is in these poems that his Romantic lyricism, his political symbolism, and his surrealistic imagery, often in an epic tone, show his real poetic self.   Regrettably, perhaps in order to give a distinctly independent identity to his style, he later began to employ some of the characteristic elements of the classical Persian prose of the eleventh and twelfth centuries which gave a pretentious archaic elegance to his poetry and, contrary to his expectation, fails to make his poetry more expressive and powerful.   In fact it is his earlier poems, especially in his second and third books, "The Fresh Air" (Havâ-ye Tâzeh) and "The Garden of Mirror" (Bâgh-e Ayeneh), with their simple but terse, powerful, vivid language, and their politico-lyrical images, that justify his reputation among his knowledgeable admirers.

On my shoulder is a dove
    that drinks from your mouth;
On my shoulder is a dove
    that refreshes my throat;
On my shoulder is a dove,
    kind and graceful,
That talks to me of light,
And of Man, who is the god of all deities ...

My bird of golden song
    nests in the foliage of your abode;
Sweetheart, put on your best dress,
Love is fond of us;
With you I follow my dreams in wakefulness,
I find my poetry in the truth of your brow.

You talk with me of light, and of Man,
who has kinship with all the gods ...
(from "I Am No Longer Alone", *The Fresh Air*)

It was his poetry in this state of lyrical surrealism with a free-flowing imagination — what we can call "Naked Poetry" — which encouraged many young poets to begin to express their immature thoughts and romantic feelings in a broken prose, which naively they expected to be appreciated as Shâmlu-esque poetry. Now there are hundreds of these poets who, with no knowledge of Persian classical and modern prosody, write prose poems devoid of any aesthetic and artistic value. Only a few of the writers of prose poems have grasped the essence of Shâmlu's style, the modernity of his vision, and the well-devised musicality of his language. Among them are Bizhan Jalâli, Tâhereh Saffârzâdeh, Esmâ'il Nuri-Alâ, Ahmad Rezâ Ahmadi, Minâ Asadi, Zhilâ Mosâ'ed, Mirzâ Âghâ Askari, and Hamid Rezâ Rahimi. Many of these poets, in the course of time, found their own poetic character and, led by Nuri-Alâ and Ahmad Rezâ Ahmadi, who were too avant-garde in their poetic outlook to stay in Shâmlu's line, formed a group called the "New Wave Poets" (Shâerân-e Mowj-e Now). Nuri-Alâ, their theoretician, insisted the "poetry remain free from social, political, or moral commitments or even commitment to conscious logic" (Ehsân Yârshâter "The Modern Literary Idiom" from *Critical Perspective on Modern Persian Literature*, edited by Thomas M. Ricks, The Three Continents Press, 1984). In the course of their experiments, the New Wave Poets took brief lessons from almost all the modernist schools of poetry which appeared in twentieth century, from Dadaism to automatism, formalism, futurism, surrealism and so on, but they failed to establish an independent, significant position in the Persian contemporary poetry.

An exception among them was Ahmad Rezâ Ahmadi, who was still a teenager when he began to publish his poems in several literary magazines. His strangely new imagery, his emphatic disregard for anything conventional in the Persian poetry, including rhythm and rhyme, his rather automatic way of writing — and especially his inventive attempts in breaking the ordinary or natural relationship between nouns and verbs, so that they could follow his surrealistic vision — made his poetry altogether chaotic and nonsensical for many, and an inspiring shock for others.

I went up blue all the stairs;
The sky of our house was not the same as our neighbour's
I went down hungry all the stairs
To the depth of wheat.

Searching for the whiteness of the horse,
All over the wheatfield, I could see only one path,
Which my father, with his grey hair, trod.

I had crossed the wheatfield alone
I had seen the wheat
But still I could not say: My horse!
They reaped my horse!

("I Only Wept the Whiteness of the Horse", 1961)

For those who did not turn away from them with a smile of disgust, Ahmadi's wild, rebellious, unyielding images were innocent messages from a young soul awakened from a dream which language, with its known order, failed to express. This order had to be broken and given a wild behaviour to find a suitable expressive harmony for that dream. In Ahmadi's poetry everything ends in sorrow, because in the world he lives in, "suspicion creates lies" and "one has to be very sincere to oneself to be able to curse the devil at the depth of one's heart." He himself, in an article entitled "Lie, Truth, and I" (*Khusheh* weekly, April 1967), wrote:

"He [the reader of his poetry] was afraid of the mist of my garden and did not enter it for a promenade and my gift [his poetry] withered in my hand, but it did not die, and I knew that some day this mist would disperse and we would find each other again ... and if the garden of my poetry is artificial, the reason is my honesty, because the reflections of time and milieu have polluted the water in my garden. Its fruits are metallic and its blossoms and birds are of paper. And what is real, are only the cages that hang on the leaden walls ... One day when the mist disappears, the birds, the fruits of poetry and life itself will become real ... and we will come out of the garden and see shining on its gates these three words: Love, Man and Life. And we will separate from each other, and on departure, instead of saying Goodbye, we will say Hello! The garden will settle in its struggle of life, and we will follow the roads to our own dreams."

Ahmadi's poetry, which became more and more obscure by his abandoning the syntactic and logical order of the Persian language, deprived him of a place among the prominent modernist poets; but it did encourage many poets to break the boundaries of familiar and hackneyed imagery and enter a new realm of poetic vision. Among these, poets of an older generation were Yadollâh Royâ'i, Sohrâb Sepehri and Forugh Farrokhzâd.

Royâ'i, who was first a follower of Tavallali in his poetic experiments, later showed a tendency towards the style of the New Wave. But paying more attention to form than to subject matter, he began to attack the involvement of poetry with any ideology or commitment and, with a number of younger artists and poets, formed a group called "Spacementalists". The goal in Spacementalism, as explained in their manifesto (published in 1961 in *Barresi-ye Ketâb*, a monthly book review) was to search "for the absolute, immediate, impatient perceptions beyond the realities". It was "absolute, because it is risen from the existentialist aspect of reality and from its ultimate cause." Their manifesto also said: "Spacementalist poetry escapes from the lies of ideology and the business of commitment; and as far as responsibility is concerned, [a Spacementalist poet] is only responsible for his own work and his inner self, which is revolutionary and awake." They believed that "between reality and ultra-reality there exists a 'space', and for reaching the perception, the poet must be quick in crossing this space, without leaving any footprints. It means that we do not see his act of jumping over the space, but we encounter him only when he, with his perception of the world beyond reality, has returned to our world of reality, and what we see is this perception." (Esmâ'il Nuri-Alâ, *Theory of Poetry*, Qazal Publications, London, 1994)

> I cross the beyond, and I do not catch the beyond
> When the beyond is traversed
> The swift beauties of miles
> Traverse my steps
> And somewhere else, in another beyond
> They sleep with the virgin distances.
> At the time of traversing the beyond
> The empty hand says to the traversed steps:
> Then where do lie the tame beyond?
> (Yadollâh Royâ'i, *Labial Verses*)

Forugh Farrokhzâd, who had published three books of poems, *The Captive* (Asir), *The Wall* (Divâr), and *Rebellion* (Osyân), was influenced for a good part of her poetical life by a number of different poets, especially Tavallali, Nâderpur, Nosrat Rahmâni, and later, Yadollâh Royâ'i. But in subject matter, she was daring and brave enough to express the hidden feelings and emotions of the Iranian women who had been suffering a double repression, deprived of many civil and even of some fundamental human rights in a patriarchal, Muslim society. Her earlier poems were weak in form and without much originality in imagery, but they clearly reflected the sorrows and the aspirations of contemporary Iranian young women, who felt "drowned in [their] innocent youth" and confined to a repressed life behind the curtains of traditions. She knew that young women like her wished to free themselves from the prison of veiled chastity and forced modesty, and to shout out, among other things, their natural desires:

> I want you, and I know
> That I can never take you in my arms;
> You are like that clear, bright sky,
> And I am a captive bird in this cage.
>   ("The Captive", *Selected Poems*)

Her first step of rebellion in real life was to separate from her husband, whom she had married at the age of sixteen as arranged by her parents. Being a divorced mother at the age of nineteen, it was very agonizing for her to pass through this stage of liberation. In a poem entitled "The Demon of the Night", reproaching her for the sin she has committed, the evil spirit of darkness, says to her: "I am a demon, but you are a worse demon than I!/ A mother, and yet unchaste? Oh! how dare you to let the poor pure child/ lay his head on your stained lap!" And then, in another poem entitled "The Deserted Home", she admits that, by leaving her husband and her only child, she has deprived their home of "the happiness of life" and says: "I know that now a child is crying,/ full of sorrow of separation from his mother;/ But, wounded at heart and distressed, I am on the path of my desire./ My friend and my beloved is poetry/ And I go to find it."

The second great step Farrokhzâd took, this time in her artistic life, was to free herself from the fascinating influence of the romantic Neo-classicist poets, and even of imitating Nimâ Yushij's innovations in rhythm and style. In an interview published in the literary periodical *Ârash*, and reprinted as a foreword to her *Selected Poems*, she had said: "He [Nimâ Yushij] was my guide, but I was the maker of myself. I have always relied on my own experiments. I should have discovered how Nimâ managed to reach his new language and form . If I had not discovered this, I would have come to nothing. I would have become an imitator without consciousness. I should have made my own journey, that is to say I should have lived my life."

When her rebellion against traditional values, social old norms and hypocritical religious restrictions had gone far enough to give her the freedom of personality for which she had long fought, Forugh Farrokhzâd began her real journey in the realm of selfhood. It was then that she stopped writing poems which were the plain cries of an unhappy woman, despised by society, and sometimes very close to erotica:

31

In the silence of the temple of desire
I am lying beside your passionate body;
My kisses have left their marks on your shoulders
Like fiery bites of a snake."
                    ("The Song of Beauty", *Rebellion*)

It was then that she was born again, both in her world view and in her poetry.   Her friendship with a number of modernist poets and erudite intellectuals, like Yadollâh Royâ'i, Ahmad Shâmlu, Ebrâhim Golestân, Parviz Dâriyush, and Ahmad Rezâ Ahmadi, encouraged her to find a quite different poetical vision.   Now she could say: "poetry is a serious matter for me.   It is a responsibility which I feel I have to my own individuality.   It is some sort of answer which I should give to my life."   From then on, instead of standing against society, she tried to understand it; instead of being the voice of her individual world, she became conscious of the great common spirit of mankind.   Her poems, while simple and fluid in their language and imagery, found a new depth and a rather philosophical tone.

They were drowned in their own fear
And the frightening sense of sin
Had paralysed
Their blind, dumb souls ...

Perhaps
Behind their crushed eyes, at the depth of inanimateness,
Something confused, with a flicker of life,
Was still left;
And, with its faint effort,
It wanted to believe in the purity of the waters' songs.

Perhaps; but what an infinite emptiness!
The sun was dead,
And no one knew
That the name of the sad dove,
Which had escaped from hearts, was Faith.
                    ("The Earthly Verses", *Born Again*)

In her poems of this new period, rhyme lost its aesthetic function and what replaced it was the music felt in the meaning of verbs, which in Persian usually come at the end of the sentences (in her case at the end of lines and stanzaic paragraphs), and also, here and there, the prominence of nouns, adjectives and adverbs.   In other words, she did not want to break the melodic flow of her sentences or lines with the repeated hammering of rhymes. As for rhythm, she began to use broken metres, sometimes letting a line lose the metre in one or two syllables, and then regain it. It may or may not have been deliberate, but it gives a fresh tone to the music of her poems, which is rather the music of thought than of words. Life, death, happiness, sorrow, the beauty of nature, the ugliness of social injustice, hope in love's triumph, despair caused by the force of ignorance and hypocrisy, and other notions and emotions, filled her poems with the spirit of reality, and still, now and then, she returned to the most powerful and the subtlest virtue of her poetic vision: the sacredness of womanhood and the mystical beauty of sex.

> ... The clock flew away,
> The curtain went away with the wind;
> I had squeezed him
> In the halo of fire;
> I wanted to speak
> But, ohh!
> His dense shady eyelashes
> Like the fringes of a silk curtain
> Flowed from the depth of darkness
> Along the stretched groin of desire,
> Along the quiver, that deadly quiver,
> Down the lost end of mine.
>
> I felt I was being freed,
> I felt I was being freed.
>
> I felt my skin burst in the expansion of love;
> I felt my fiery mass melt slowly,
> And then it trickled,
>   trickled,
>   trickled
> Down into the moon, the sunken, agitated dark moon.
>   ("Union", *Born Again*)

In 1967, about four years after the publication of *Born Again*, Farrokhzâd, who was happily enjoying her new life, died in a car accident. Her next book, *Let Us Believe in the Beginning of the Cold Season*, was published in 1975. On the strength of these two books she found a place among the great contemporary poets who have had an important role in the evolution of contemporary Persian poetry with their modernistic experiments in form, style and poetic perspective. But like Shâmlu, whose prose poems encouraged hundreds of ungifted young people to become "poets" overnight, Farrokhzâd's simplicity of style, colloquial fluidity of language and naked, strange but powerful imagery, opened the way for an outpouring of pseudo-Farrokhzâdesque hallucinational and absurd verses. Mehdi Akhavân Sâless ("M. Omid"), one of Iran's best-known modernist poets, in a long critical appendix to his fifth book of poems, *From This Avestâ*, while admiring Farrokhzâd for her successful new experiments, angrily criticized her untalented imitators:

"And sometimes I have thought that, perhaps, occasionally, the case of the *lady of our time*, Forugh Khânom ... in some of her recent works is different. I greet her and say to her: "Well done, damsel! One lock of your curly tresses — though you have cropped them very short in the European style and *à la garçon* — is worth more than a flock of those *hermaphrodites* whom we know; and then I remember, and it makes me laugh, that since this prodigious lady has produced some works of good quality (and as she herself has said, she was born again after the age of thirty or forty), how the situation of the poetry market ... suddenly changed; how everybody ... gave up or changed their own chaotic, haphazard styles ... and they all tried to take the guise of a gazelle, though, I beg your pardon for being rude, they actually had the figure of a mule. They all limpingly followed the path of bumpy metres ... and they wrote such strange things that God alone knows what they are! And, in the domain of imagery, they suddenly began to *cry inside the mirror* in the day time and to *see bogeys through the window at night;* they all *stood at the side of the street and watched the fountains;* they recited dark and bright *earthly verses* on the divinity of bread; and if they had not felt ashamed of their sexual identity ... they would have *become pregnant under the red rose bushes ...*" (*From This Avestâ*, pp. 179-80 — the phrases given in italics are satirical references to certain images in some of Farrokhzâd's poems).

However, Farrokhzâd's influence on many women poets, among them Shâdâb Vajdi, Maimanat Mir-Sâdeghi (Âzâdeh), Zhilâ Mosâ'ed, Minâ Asadi, and others, was inspiring and constructive. Her poetic vision has continued to be one of the achievements of modernism in Persian poetry.

But Mehdi Akhavân Sâless, who was among the most zealous supporters of Nimâ Yushij's innovations and wrote two books explaining and justifying them, made his own modernistic experiments based on a deep knowledge of Persian classical poetry. Before coming to Tehran from his native city, Mashad (in the province of Khorâsân, the cradle of Persian literature in the eleventh to fifteenth centuries), he wrote ghazals and ghasidehs in the traditional style with remarkable skill. After some experiments in the Nimâ-esque style, his personal poetic diction, matured by the absorption of the great classical works and enriched with the Khorâsâni dialect of Persian, took him back to what was his own Neo-classical style. Like some of the works of the old masters, his poetry mixes the order and the flow of the spoken language with the structure of an elevated style, using colloquial words and expressions along with archaic ones in such skilful way that the result seems quite natural. This gives an interesting, sometimes witty, tone to his poems. In 1968, in a long interview with Sirus Tâhbâz, (the editor of *Daftarhâ-ye Zamâneh*, a literary periodical), Shafi'i Kadkani and Esmâ'il Kho'i, he said:

"I try to graft the healthy, sound nerves and veins of the pure living language—which bring all its dynamic elements and its strong skeleton from the past—on to today's blood, feelings and pulse (as far as I can succeed in such a surgical mediation). It is for this reason that I employ everything from the past which is acceptable and good to be developed; everything still useful, alive and active; the words which are full of meaning, and have special intrinsic elegance ... I depend upon a thousand years of Persian literature ..."

Akhavân Sâless has been particularly successful in his narrative poems, which have a pronounced musical quality with many puns, rhymes and inter-rhymes, as well as a tone which sounds like a deliberate accompaniment of lyric melodies with the drum beats of an epic voice. Of course, his excessive interest in using rhymes produces many lines which, though beautiful in themselves, are superfluous and, in some cases, overshadow the main theme. Akhavân Sâless lives in a gloomy, despairing "present" which is seen in the light of the glorious, beautiful "past" of his nation. It is a "present" full of nostalgia for historical and mythical figures and events. In his lamentations over the successive destructions and adversities caused by foreign invaders, Akhavân Sâless is the living memory of a long history. In his vision the ancient Iranian Empire with its great Cyruses and Dariuses, and its great native religions: Mithraism, Zoroastrianism, Zervanism, Manichaeism and Mazdakism, lies in the background of its humbled, mournful present.

However, Akhavân Sâless is not completely occupied in his mind and heart with nationalistic sorrows and aspirations. In some of his longer poems, his consciousness finds a wider expanse beyond the small unreal world he has made for himself with the ruins of an ancient history, and lets him see the real big world and the whole mankind:

Hey! Where is it?
Where is the capital of this chaotic, malevolent century;

This century of fiendish ridicule,
Which in the conquest of the space has gone beyond the moon,
But has fallen off the orbit of the sun of love;
The bloodthirsty century,
The century of the most horrible messages,
The century in which with the droppings of a high-flying, unreal bird
They throw in ruins the *Four Pillars* of God's *Seven Regions* in a
                                                    moment ...

Where is the capital of this shameless, faithless century
In which, without the least pity
Every new blossom is given to the wind of death,
As is exposed to denial, contempt, betrayal and injustice
The proper reverence of the old trees, now having passed the last
                                        season of their fruitfulness ...
            ("The End of the Shâhnâmeh" from a book with the same title)

While Ahmad Shâmlu was able to have a wide influence on a majority
of younger poets with his modern and rather Eluardian poetic vision and by
abandoning Persian traditional metres and writing in a musical prose, Mehdi
Akhavân Sâless had little to offer to younger poets in term of poetic vision.
It was only his narrative language with its epic tone and descriptive style
which could attract some of the poets, especially those who were from his own
province, Khorâsân and already familiar with that characteristic of his diction
which is formed and enriched by the Khorâsâni Persian. The most successful
of these poets is Esmâ'il Kho'i, whose earlier poems were imitative, but who
later, developed a much more powerful and versatile style which could be
used for different themes — from simple, pure lyrical emotions to profound
philosophical concepts.   One original, and in many cases successful,
characteristic of his longer poems is the division of parts of sentences into very
long hemstitches. This gives a flow like that of spoken word to the whole
poem, and makes it particularly suitable for recitation.

Kho'i studied philosophy in England, and is especially impressed by
Friedrich Nietzsche among the European philosophers. He is a keen observer
of Nature and a meditating traveller in the realm of Self. What he discovers
in Nature and Self, is different from what he sees in the world today, in the
relation of man to man and of man to nature, and it makes him sad, it makes
him angry. Though he is not a revolutionary poet like young Mayakovsky,
but more a romantic like Holderlin and his desire is to be at one with the
cosmos, again and again he warns the forces of injustice in society of an
inevitable red revolution:

The red moment
      — which you must know —
         is on its way.
Sooner or later
An anger from hell would say:
      "Fire!"
("Along the Khaki March of the Street", *The Poems*, Vol. I,)

Yet the poet in him, in his most sincere voice, is a philosophizing lyricist who feels himself "to be so like a sublime poem, an exuberant, humane poem, that words know him as their own primeval meaning, their eternal echo, and they sing their bright and dark songs in him, like the spring and autumn which sing their songs through the throats of canaries and turtle-doves." ("With the Lip Sealed" *Poems*, Vol. I). In his solitude, when he is free from the social and political concerns, he returns to real freedom and says, as if to himself and not to the readers of his poetry:

What I see
Is the permanence of the sea;
The journey of the night towards the day;
It is not the transience of the waves, flowers and dewdrops.
Though we pass away,
The way will remain;
      there is no reason for regret.
("On the Way", *Poems*, Vol. I)

However, as far as Kho'i's poetry is concerned, I think there is one reason for regret because — after the Islamic Revolution in Iran when, disillusioned and angry, he left the country — like many other Iranian poets and writers he began to use his artistic power to fight against the religious regime, and many of his poems became too politicized and lost their transparent artistic sincerity, universality of vision and unbounded imaginative power. Yet Esmâ'il Kho'i, with his first seven books of poems, which were published before the 1979 Revolution, will always be remembered as one of the outstanding modernist poets of his time.

Another poet of Kho'i's generation, and like him from the province of Khorâsân, who is supposed to be influenced by the language, style and poetic vision of Akhavân Sâless, is Mohammad Rezâ Shafi'i Kadkani ("M. Sereshk"). But his poetry, often tinctured with symbolic political messages, has the main characteristics of Hushang Ebtehâj's new romantic lyricism. Both of them owe the smooth, melodic texture of their language and their stylized visual imagery to Hâfez and both of them, especially Ebtehâj, are closer to Tavallali in their conception of modernity than to Nimâ Yushij. What they write in new forms, with lines of different lengths and with new arrangements of rhymes, are in essence classical ghazals. If modern intellectualism in Iran was not so widely identified with political and ideological commitment, poets like Hushang Ebtehâj, Shafi'i Kadkani and Siyavâsh Kasrâ'i, with their romantic outlook, would have written pure lyrical poetry, with love, nature and beauty as their main themes. The most frequent images in their poems are protestations against repression and social injustice, symbolized as the hellish darkness of night; hope for the dawning of the day of freedom and admiration of those who give their lives for the realization of noble, humanistic cause.

In *Mirror Inside Mirror* (poems selected by Shafi'i Kadkani from Hushang Ebtehâj's nine books of poems) *night, blood, sorrow, tears* and *morning* are, respectively, the most repeated images employed by the poet. In one of his widely read poems, Ebtehâj says:

With all my anger,
With all my wild hatred,
I cry:
        O executioner!
            shame on you!

Ah! when one man kills
Another man,
He kills the essence of humanity in himself.

Listen, O executioner!
There will eventually dawn
A different day:
The day of justice,
        the day of revenge,
The day when this land, dressed with blood
            will have to yield ...
            ("On the Cobblestones of the Road", *Mirror Inside Mirror*)

The book in which this poem was first published in mid-summer 1953, was banned soon after the Shah's *coup d' état*, but almost all the intellectuals, especially the Communists and their sympathizers, expressed their anger against the Shah by repeating "O Executioner, shame on you!" This and a few other poems like it were enough to make their creator popular — as also had been the case with Shafi'i Kadkani's book, *Of Being and Singing*, first published in 5000 copies and reprinted within two months in another 20,000:

> The millennial of sleep,
> The great celebration of the swamp.
>
> O you, the frogs of filthy waters, the eaters of slime!
> Beyond this long lingering but not everlasting spell
> There shines the sun of a burning truth
> Which will dry your small shallow swamp ...
>
> Yet
> All this jubilant commotion of yours,
> In the eye of the truth, is futile;
> A real mourning, festive in appearance,
> For your chastisement,
> The sunny days will dawn;
> They are late, but they are not too far away.
> ("Late, but not Far Away", *Of Being and Singing*)

Among those poets who first were excited by Nimâ Yushij's innovations but soon preferred Tavallali's moderate changes in form and style, Nâder Nâderpur has been the most successful. Apart from his skill in using the classical metres in free verse, Nâderpur has enriched his lyrical perception by his clear understanding of the spirit of lyricism in the works of great masters, from Rudaki to Mowlavi, Sa'di and Hâfez. Like Nimâ Yushij and Shâmlu, he made himself familiar with the poetry of the French Romanticists and Symbolists. William Rees, in his book, *French Poetry, 1820-1950* (Penguin, 1990) says about the Romantic movement in France: "The new spirit encouraged a preoccupation with the self, its sensibilities, its sufferings and its dreams with love, its ecstasies, its uncertainties and its torments; with time, death and eternity ..." If this can be accepted as a description of Romanticism, Nâderpur is a Romantic, with an obsessive indulgence in themes of love and its pleasures, which sometimes finds expression in an adolescent type of desire:

> O, master matador of all ages,
> Hold up your crimson satin skirt
> Always in front of my eyes
> To enrage the powerful bull of lust in me ...
> The bull whose thick horn will leave a burning wound
> Between your thighs;
> The bull that in its agony of death

Will throw a jet of blood towards you.
May its blood change into honey and wine in you, O, Woman!
The master matador of all ages!

("Spanish Game", *Blood and Ashes*)

Again, with an obvious exaggeration about the *ennui* of life, if asked "what was there in life for which he would live for", he would have no answer but admitting that "because he was afraid of death, he had no other choice but living." In spite of all this pessimism, Nâderpur excels in describing the ecstasy of desire, the glory of love, and in adoring woman as the embodiment of all the beauty in nature — which can be interpreted as a lust for life. As for his social outlook, it was only after the Islamic Revolution in Iran that his anger against the theocratic regime made him write a number of political poems. Ehsân Yârshâter, in his essay "The Modern Literary Idiom" divides the contemporary Iranian poets into the *Committed* and the *Uncommitted*, and puts Nâderpur among the *Nonpolitical* or the *Uncommitted* poets. But Nâderpur himself has a different thing to say about "commitment" for a poet. In his foreword to his seventh book of poems, *The Last Supper*, he writes: "in my opinion, if what is meant by 'commitment' is to write about the temporary political issues and social daily events, then it certainly is contrary to the vocation of a poet, which is breaking through the boundaries of time and attain eternity ... Moreover, to be a committed poet does not mean that he should never speak about himself, and that only about people as a whole is he committed to speak; in other words he should replace "I" with "We". If the work of a poet would be devoid of insight and originality, this change of pronouns would mean nothing but deceit ... If a poet often speaks in the first person, it does not mean that he ignores others. More often than not by speaking of himself, he speaks for all ..."

Nevertheless, after the Islamic Revolution, Nâderpur, like Fereydun Moshiri and Simin Behbahâni, has let his political discontent, resulting from the depressing situation in Iran, play an important role in his poetry, sometimes degrading a poem to the level of an angry slogan:

Oh, the devil incarnate! since the tyranny of Fate
Has given you the heritage of my nation,
Your hands have sown nothing under the heart-illuminating
        sun of my homeland but the seeds of inhumanity;
It is time for me to warn you of the crop you shall reap ...
Soon the day of revenge will dawn,
And when you open your eyes

You will hear the people, old and young, common and noble men,
                                                                        shouting:
Oh, black-hearted demon!
Now your death will bring happiness to the people;
May your name be erased from the memory of time!
          (from "The Sermon of Annihilation", [For the Imam of the
          People], *Blood and Ashes*)

The regrettable fact is that since the Constitutional Revolution in 1905,
especially during the dictatorial reign of the Pahlavi dynasty, the *Pen* has been
expected to perform the duty of the *Sword*, and Persian literature, especially
poetry, has greatly suffered from this misconception. Many of the poets who
have created poems of the highest quality have given in to the public demand
and have politicized their poetry to become popular. Even a poet like Sohrab
Sepehri, who has been known as an uncommitted poet who puts art above
anything else and believes in the doctrine of *art for art's sake*, after the Islamic
Revolution became one of the favourite poets of the pro-regime religious
intellectuals. Though his mysticism is a blend of Sufism, Buddhism, and
Hindu philosophy, with a tinge of pantheism, he uses many of the Islamic
words and images, sometimes even with allusions contrary to their actual
meanings. Yet most of the readers of his poetry usually do not go deeper than
the narrow, conventional meanings of the words on which they impose their
own associative ideas and images. Here are some examples:

" How smooth is the path for the *ascension* of things ... The wind blew
from the direction of the *green* basket of *miracles* ... Open me like a door to
the *descent* of pear in this age of the *ascension* of steel ... Take the moments
to the pastures of *prophethood* ... And you, all the olive trees in the land of
Palestine,/ Address to me the abundance of your shades,/ to this lonely
traveller, who returns from a visit to *Mount Sinai,*/ And is in burning ecstasy
by *having spoken to God* ... I am, a Moslem./ My Ka'ba [Ka'beh] is a red rose/
My *prayer mat* a spring, my *prayer clay tablet* the light./ And the plain is my
place of worship/ I perform my *ablutions* with the pulses of the windowpanes./
In my prayer flows the moon, flows the spectrum./ Stones can be seen through
my prayer:/ All the particles of my prayer have crystallized./ I say my prayer/
When the wind calls as a *muezzin* on the top of the cypress' *minaret.*/ I say my
prayer as the grass repeats: *Allah is great,*/ And the *imam* of the waves lets
me know when I should rise from *prostration.*/ My Ka'ba, like a breeze, goes
from one garden to another; goes from one town to another./ My *sacred Black
Stone* is the brightness of the garden. (from "The Footsteps of Water", "The
Traveller", "The Green Mass", and "We, Nothing; We, A Glance".)

Persian mysticism, which in its Islamic form is known as Sufism, has been introduced at its best in the lyric poetry of such mystic poets as Attâr, Mowlavi and Hâfez. Mowlavi wrote more than five thousand ghazals, each of them, on average consisting of fourteen lines. In all of them the main theme is the poet's emotional, rather illuminist, perception of God as the ultimate truth and the essence of goodness and beauty. The creation is seen as the manifestation of His existence, which can also be interpreted as the unity of existence, and of love as the only spiritual relationship between man and God. In Islamic mysticism, all this is based on a few holy traditions and verses from the Koran, such as: "I was a hidden treasure, and I desired to become known. So I created the world in order to be known;" or "Whoever knoweth himself, knoweth his Lord;" or "Those who believe, have exceeding love for God". It is, therefore, understandable that such a poet should repeat his theme in different images and his images in different forms. Despite these repetitions, Mowlavi's ghazals do not lose their individual poetic beauty and freshness. But when we come to Sohrâb Sepehri's poetry, we meet an artist who has a small number of verbal motifs, inspired through a naive, or perhaps superficial, understanding of Persian and Islamic mysticism, Hindu philosophy, Buddhism and Zen Buddhism, and Taoism of Lao Tzu and Chuang Tzu. In fact, Sepehri does not use metaphors to give expression to his poetic visions, but talks in metaphors to make up poems. We must not forget that he is an artist, and his painting technique has a formative effect on his writing. The following lines are taken from his long, autobiographical poem, "The Footsteps of Water", which is also known as his masterpiece:

I went to the world's party:
I went to the plain of Sorrow,
To the garden of Gnosis,
And to the illuminated veranda of Knowledge.
I climbed up the stairs of Religion;
I went down to the alley of Scepticism,
As far as the fresh, cool air of Freedom from Want,
As far as the wet night of Affection.
I went to visit someone on the other end of love;
I went on, as far as Woman,
As far as the lamp of Pleasure,
The silence of Desire,
The soft flap of Loneliness ...

My mother was washing up the cups
In the memory of the river ...

The town was visible
Love was visible ...
The Word was visible ...
The east of sorrow of Man's Nature;
The season of roaming in the street of Woman.
The smell of loneliness in the street of Season ...
I saw the people,
I saw the cities ...
I saw the Light and the Darkness ...
And I saw Mankind in the Light, and in the Darkness ...

Sepehri, as a modern mystic in his quest for truth and journey of enlightenment, falls under the spell of an artistic formalism and, amused with the game of designing puzzles with strange metaphors, lets his poetry lose the spirit of sincerity. But another mystic poet of his generation, Bizhan Jalâli, remains artless and sincere in his existential meditation, and true to his feelings, with a childlike innocence, he professes that:

A poet is like a dove,
Flying over the darkness of the world
With its white wings,
Sometimes imagining
To have been carrying the stars
On its wings;
And sometimes thinking
That he takes the world with himself
To the heavens.

His poetry, with no rhythm or rhyme, is the simple, pure expression of his moments of despair and hope; his fascination with the beauty of nature and the pleasure of life; and his stoic resignation to the naturalness of death. In a review of Jalâli's first book, *The Days*, Mas'ud Zavârzâdeh, a former professor of literature at the University of Oregon, said; "The underlying theme of Jalâli's poems is the emotional difficulty created by living in a world which has retained only a memory of God and is suspended in a vacuum of values. The feeling of being forgotten and abandoned, on both physical and metaphysical levels, fills the atmosphere of his poems. Physical loneliness mingles with metaphysical solitude and becomes inseparable from it because in the absence of God, more an ontological frame of reference than a theological entity, man's relationship with the outside world is robbed of its ultimate significance. Hence his Khayyami celebration of the tangible and the sensuous. Jalâli's poems are influenced by the works of Persian Sufis in tone and their imagery in reference to God." ("Abandonment in Theme of Bizhan Jalâli's Free Verse", *Mideast*, October, 1965)

A poet somewhat different from others in the themes and diction of most of his typical poems is Nosrat Rahmâni. After the Shah's *coup d'état* in 1953, Rahmâni became something of a guru in pessimism and nihilistic despair for a group of younger poets, both in their poetry and in their way of life. He talked openly of his addiction to heroin and opium in some of his poems and even wrote his memoirs in a book entitled *The Man Who Was Lost in the Dust*. By *dust* he meant *powder*, and powder was slang name given to heroin. In his pessimism there was more anger against repression and injustice than utter submission to a despair which for him came from the futility of life and the blind cruelty of fate. He called himself the "Infamous poet of the Town" and his poetic diction was based for the most part on the real life of the common people. He permitted the names of ordinary objects of daily life to enter the scene of his poetry, certain words which were considered "unpoetical" and still rarely to be found in the works of other poets today. The actual narrator in his poems of those years is Rahmâni himself as a rebellious, bohemian intellectual son of those common people. It was blasphemy, immorality, and, to some extent, love of horror and decay, as in Charles Baudelaire's *Les Fleurs du Mal*, that became the special features of his poetry. In one of his books, *Cashmere* [Termeh], he begins his foreword, addressed to his readers, with this sentence: "Let us follow our hope as far as Hell!" and he ends it with this message: "For you, my readers, I have brought no present but the talisman of calamity and despair! But if you are on your way to Hell, take my poems with you!"

However, by the late 1960's and early 1970's, the social and political situation in Iran had changed a lot. The Shah's grandiose economical and social programmes failed to satisfy the new generation of intellectuals who wanted nothing less than the change of regime and the establishment of a real democratic government in the country. In his pompous celebrations of the 2500th anniversary of the Persian Empire, standing in front of Cyrus the Great's tomb, the Shah felt sufficiently self-confident to address the spirit of the founder of the Achemenid dynasty, saying: "O, Cyrus, rest in peace, for we are awake!". At the same time revolutionary members of different underground movements were ready to give their lives to overthrow him. Though the regime thought it had succeeded in depriving the intellectuals of all the tribunes of free speech, the mosques against which he was not able to fight openly, became active in attracting people to the voices of discontent. That was how, in that period, even Marxism tactically appeared in the guise of religion. In such a situation as this, the real readers of poetry, who were mostly middle class intellectuals and university students, were not interested in the passive anger and the morbid pessimism of poets like Nosrat Rahmâni, or the sentimental love poems written by poets like Fereydun Moshiri and Simin Behbahâni. Once again "Poetry" which was known as the "symbolic language of political dissidence" had to resign itself to social commitment. Even a minor poet, who was not skilful enough to make powerful but safe symbols in his political poems, would rarely escape the keen eyes of the "symbologists" of such organisations as SAVAK (Organization for Security and Information), and was sure to be put into prison. There were even poets who deliberately used "unsafe" images and symbols, because they were eager to be arrested for the honour and fame which they could gain through "imprisonment". Only a number of experienced poets, well-equipped with the craftsmanship of "political symbolization", succeeded in giving their readers the poetry they wanted and at the same time keeping the "inquisitors" at bay.

As was mentioned earlier, the sociopolitical situation in Iran since, at least, the beginning of twentieth century has had a strange effect in literature. While it has led to the creation of the finest examples of political poetry, it has also been a great hindrance to the independence and freedom of poets in creating poetry as pure literature. To give a clear idea of the importance of the role poetry has played in political movements in Iran, suffice it to say that the most remarkable political event which took place in Iran against the repressive regime and heralded the downfall of the Shah was "The Nights of Poets and Writers", organized by the Syndicate of Iranian Writers at the Goethe Institute, the West German cultural centre in Tehran, from 10 to 20 October 1977. For the first time in about 26 years, writers delivered speeches against censorship and for freedom of expression of ideas, and poets read their poems, most of which had never been seen in print. Some poets, who were known as the "uncommitted" or non-political poets, were given a very unfriendly welcome, just as if they had committed a grave crime. No wonder that when the Revolution found an Islamic face and the secular intellectuals became disillusioned with it, many of the poets who felt that there was no place for the uncommitted poets in the new literary scene (no matter how famous they had been before) began to write political poems. But now, of course, with symbols and allusions in which the *Pulpit* had been given the place of the *Throne*.

At the height of the 1979 Revolution, I visited Aḥmad Shâmlu in Croydon, where he lived for some time before going to the United States and returning to Iran. I remember that he told me in a very nostalgic tone: "In these days I cannot write poems. My style, my language, my symbols, all had been taken form in the time of repression and censorship. Now that I am free to say what I want, I have no poetical language for it." And to his relief, soon the situation changed and the new regime appeared with a much harsher repression and much severer censorship, and Shâmlu found the opportunity again to put to use the same old style of political symbolism:

> They smell your mouth
> To find out if you have told someone:
> *I love you!*
> They smell your heart!
> Such a strange time it is, my dear;
> And they punish Love
> At thoroughfares
> By flogging.
> > *We must hide our love in dark closets ...*
> > ("In This Dead End", *The Small Songs of Exile*, 1990)

According to Mehdi Akhavân Sâless, in an interview in 1968, Nimâ Yushij had experienced the same disadvantage of political symbolization in poetry before Ahmad Shâmlu:

"Well, because of the political situation in the period between 1921 and 1941 [the despotic reign of Rezâ Shah], his [Nimâ Yushij's] poetry had become indirect, symbolic and mysterious for many years. Writing this type of poetry had become his technique ... But there came a time [after Rezâ Shah's abdication, and for several years after World War II] when the nature of events required more clarity and openness in expression. The reasons for writing in a symbolical language did not exist any more. Nimâ was very dissatisfied with this habit-breaking change; but after several years, when the situation returned to what it had been before 1941, with similar restrictions, one day I heard him saying: 'Well, how wonderful! Now one can write again those mysterious, symbolical poems ... Now one can easily say things in one's poems which none of the inspectors and security officers can understand!' "

In many cases what the "inspectors of literature", the censors, thought they had understood, was a clear indication of their misinterpretations. One of my own poems, in which I had tried to metaphorize the mystery of life with all its ferocious innocence and painful beauty, was interpreted by some of the censors as an ode in praise of the leader of a small group of guerrillas who had their base in a forest in a northern province. They were betrayed by the locals, captured by the security forces and executed. In the atmosphere of suppression, any simple image could be taken as a symbol for something that inspired fear in the regime. The censors had found a number of such images in my poem, entitled "The Prayer of Love":

> He walks through the *forest*
> Brimful of the affection of *rain*,
> But with the *wrath* of *earthquake*.
>
> In his eyes the *vision* of the blossoms of *fire*
> Reflected in the eyes of *water*.
> In his mind
> The *tumult* of a sudden growth
> Of a hundred *forests of deer*.
>
> With every *footfall* of his
> A great *battle* fought,
> And of the *bodies* of the *slain*
> Heaps and heaps left behind,
> All in a deep ecstasy of coition.
>
> The general of the wild
> *Is coming through the forest*
> With the *pride* of a *young lover*,
> And his *beloved*, the *deer*,
> In her eyes the simple *dawn* of shyness
> Mixed with the *shadow of fear*
> Terribly restless for his *arrival*:
> Behold!
> *The claws of the conqueror*
> And *the heart of the conquered*;
> Now:
> The *prayer of love*
> In the *temple of nature*.

The politicisation of literature in Iran has been the natural reaction of writers and poets to prolonged dictatorial rule, blind suppression, and absurd censorship. As its positive result, it has helped some of the highly talented poets to create many brilliant political poems. Its negative result has been to narrow the scope of poetical vision for the poets, as well as for the readers — so much so that the majority of readers, if they cannot find some familiar political images in the first few lines of a poem, hardly care to finish reading it. For this reason, few have been the poets who could deny themselves the joy of popularity in order to create profound poetry with a universal perspective and power and originality of thought and imagination. Of all the works of the most famous and most popular poets, only a small selection may survive as poetry *par excellence*.

After the Islamic Revolution, censorship found new dimensions and poems with new political symbols and images reached a higher level of popularity. During the last sixteen years many other young poets have appeared, most of whom write crude, unaesthetic prose poems. There is also a group of poets who, influenced by the politicized Islamic idealism and encouraged by the Islamic regime, employ such classical forms as ghazal, ghasideh and masnavi (rhymed couplets) for their mystical, religious and political themes. So far one cannot see among them anyone of promise. But Persian poetry, with a heritage of more than a thousand years will pass through this period of decline, as it did at the beginning of this century, when it came out of its old, closed world and gave scope to creative talents to pursue a universal vision.

Mahmud Kianush

London, July 1995

NOTES ON THE POETS
AND THEIR WORK

Nimâ Yushij, pen name of Ali Esfadiyâri, b. 1895, Yush village, Mâzandarân; d. 1969, Tehran.   Most of his poems were published posthumously in book forms.

Poetical Works: Mâkh-Ulâ River [Mâkh-ulâ,1965]; My Poetry [She're Man, 1966]; Church Bell [Nâghus, 1966]; The Town of Night & The Town of Morning [Shahr-e Shab va Shahr-e Sobh, 1967]; Scribblings [Ghalam-andâz, 1970]; Other Cries & The Spider of Colour [Faryâdhâ-ye Digar & Ankabut-e Rang, 1971]; Water in the Ants' Nest [Âb dar Khâbgah-e Murchegân, a collection of quatrains, 1972]; Fantasy [Afsâneh, 1922, a long lyrico-dramatic poem]; Mâneli & Sarivili' House [Mâneli & Khâneh-ye Sarivili, 1973, two long narrative poems]; Anecdotes & The Soldier's Family [Hekâyât & Khânevâdeh-ye Sarbâz, 1974, a number of didactic anecdotes and a long narrative poem]; The Complete Poetical Works [Majmu'e-ye Ash'âr, 1991]. The best-known of his other works is *The Neighbour's Words* [Harfhâ-ye Hamsâyeh, 1971], the poet's letters to an imaginary young poet in explanation of his views about the principles and the spirit of modernity in poetry. He also wrote several stories for children.

Fereydun Tavallali, b. 1919 Shirâz; d. 1985 Shirâz.

Poetical Works: Unchained [Rahâ, 1950]; Musk Bag [Nâfeh, 1962]; Trot [Puyeh, 1966].

Shahnâz A'lâmi, b. 1921, Esfahân.   In 1954, one year after the Shah's *coup d'état* and overthrow of Mosaddegh's government, she left Iran and resided in former East Germany.   Currently she lives in Berlin and runs an Iranian School.

Poetical Works: Cham Village [Dehkadeh-ye Cham, 1985, Germany]; Songs of Separation [Taranehâ-ye Jodâ'i, 1991, Germany]; Mr. Now Ruz and Miss Manizheh [Now Ruz Aghâ va Manizheh Khânom, 1970, a story in verse for children]. She has also written biographical sketches and a critical work on women's role in Persian literature.

Zhâleh Esfahâni, also known as "Zhâleh Soltâni" and "Zhâleh"; b. 1921, Esfahân.   She left Iran in 1947 and lived in the former Soviet Union until her return to Iran in 1979, after the Revolution.   Currently she lives in London.

Poetical Works: Wild Flowers, [Golhâ-ye Khod-ru, 1945]; The Living River [Zendeh Rud, the name of a river in Esfahân, 1965, Moscow]; The Blue Ship [Kashti-ye Kabud, 1972, Tajikistan]; The Image of the World [Naghsh-e Jahân, Moscow, 1980]; If I had a Thousand Pens [Agar Hezâr Ghalam Midâshtam, 1991]; The Invincible Elburz [Alborz-e Bi-shekast, London, 1983]; O the Favourable Wind! [Ey Bâd-e Shorteh!, London 1983].   She also wrote Persian translations of a selection of foreign poets and critical works on Malek-osh-Sho'arâ Bahâr and Nimâ Yushij.

Manucher Sheybâni, b. 1923, Tehran; d. 1991, Tehran.   He was also a well-known artist.

Poetical Works: Spark [Jaraghgheh, 1945]; The Extinguished Fire Temple [Âtashkadeh-ye Khâmush, 1963]; Desert Mirages [Sarâbhâ-ye Kaviri]. He also wrote several other dramatic works.

Ahmad Shâmlu, also known by his pen name "A. Bâmdâd"; b. 1925, Tehran.

Poetical Works: The Forgotten Songs [Âhanghâ-ye Farâmush Shodeh, 1947]; Resolution [Ghat'nâmeh, 1957]; The Garden of Mirror [Bâgh-e Âyeneh, 1962]; Âydâ in the Mirror & Moments and Eternity [Âydâ dar Ayeneh va Lahzehâ va Hamisheh, 1964]; Âydâ, Trees, Dagger and Memory

[Âydâ, Derakht, Khânjar va Khâtereh, 1965]; Phoenix Under the Rain [Ghoghnus dar Bârân, 1966]; Elegies of the Earth [Marsiyehâ-ye Khâk,1969]; Blossoming in the Mist [Shekoftan dar Meh, 1970]; Abraham amid the Fire [Ebrâhim dar Atash, 1993]; A Poniard in the Plate [Deshneh dar Dis,1973]; Little Songs of Exile [Taranehâ-ye Kuchek-e Ghorbat, 1980]. Other works include several stories for children, and many essays and translations.

Esmâ'il Shâhrudi, also known by his pen name "Âyandeh"; b. 1925, Dâmghân; d. 1981, Tehran.

Poetical Works: The Last Battle [Âkherin Nabard, with an introduction by Nimâ Yushij,1951]; Future [Âyandeh, 1967]; "... and With Wine Fill the Gob..." [... m va Mey dar Sâ ..., 1970; The title of the book is a broken phrase from a well-known line from Hafez: Let us break the dome of the heavens and with wine fill the goblet]; In every Direction Road, Road, Road [Har Suy Râh, Râh, Râh, 1971]; O the Dweller of the Meeting Place! [Ây Mighât-Neshin!, 1975].

Fereydun Moshiri, b. 1925, Tehran.

Poetical Works: Thirsty for Tempest [Teshneh-ye Tufân, 1955]; The Sea's Fault [Gonâh-e Daryâ, 1956]; The Unfound [Nâyâfteh, 1958]; Cloud [Abr, 1959]; Cloud ... and the Alley [Abr ... va Kucheh, 1964]; Believe in the Spring [Bahâr râ Bâvar Kon, 1968]; Flight with the Sun [Parvâz bâ Khorshid, 1982]; Of Silence [Az Khâmushi, 1977]; The Pearl of Love [Morvarid-e Mehr, 1984]; Ah, Rain! [Ah, Bârân, 1985]; From the Land of Reconciliation [Az Diyâr-e Âshti, 1992].

Siyâvash Kasrâ'i, also known by his pen name, Kowli, meaning "gipsy"; b. 1926, Esfahân, d. 1996. He left Iran some time after the Islamic Revolution, when the government turned against the Communist Party and put many of its leaders into prison, and died in Vienna on 8 February 1996.

Poetical Works: Voice [Âvâ, 1955]; Ârash the Archer [Ârash-e Kamângir, a long narrative poem, 1957]; Siyâvash's Blood [Khun-e Siyâvash, 1963]; With the Extinct Damâvand [Bâ Damâvand-e Khâmush, 1966]; Stone and Dew [Sang va Shabnam, 1966, lyrical quatrains]; Domesticated [Khânegi, 1967]; With the Redness of Fire, with the Taste of Smoke [Be Sorkhi-ye Âtash, be Ta'm-e Dud, 1978]; It Is Not the Time of Silence [Vaght-e Sokut Nist, 1978]; From the Beginning of the Curfew Until Dawn [Az Ghorogh tâ Khoruskhân, 1979]; The Red Bead [Mohre-ye-Sorkh, a long poem, Austria, 1995]. Other works include several stories for children and young adults.

Mohammad Zohari, b. 1926, Shahsavâr, Mâzandarân; d. 1995, Tehran. After the Islamic Revolution he left Iran and lived in Paris. In 1989 he returned to Iran.

Poetical Works: The Island [Jazireh, 1955]; Gelâyeh [Complaint, 1956]; Clandestine Paper [Shabnâmeh, 1958]; And the Rest [Va Tatemmeh, 1959]; Fists in Pockets [Mosht dar Jib, 1962]; Thus Said Our Master [Pir-e Mâ Goft, 1979].

Nosrat Rahmâni, b. 1927, Tehran.

Poetical Works: Migration [Kuch, 1970]; Desert [Kavir, 1970]; Cashmere [Termeh, 1968]; Rendezvous in Slime [Mi'âd dar Lajan, 1967]; The Wind on Fire [Harigh-e Bâd, 1970]; Reaping [Derow, 1972]; Sword, Beloved of Pen [Shamshir, Ma'shugheh-ye Ghalam, 1989]; Wine Passed Another Round [Piyâleh Dowr-e Degar Zad, 1990]. Other works include *The*

Man Who Was Lost in the Dust [Mardi Keh dar Ghobâr Gom Shod, 1959, memoirs of the poet as an addict], and several short stories.

Bizhan Jalâli, born, 1927, Tehran.
Poetical Works: Days [Ruzhâ, 1964]; Our Heart and the World [Del-e Mâ va Jahân, 1968]; The Colour of the Waters [Rang-e Abhâ,1969]; Water and the Sun [Âb va Âftab, 1987]; A Diary [Ruzânehâ, 1990].

Simin Behbahâni, b. 1928, Tehran.
Poetical Works: The Broken Lute [Seh-târ-e Shekasteh, 1951; the tar is a Persian musical instrument with five strings, and seh-tar is a type of Tar with three strings]; Footprint [Jâ-ye Pâ, 1954]; Candelabrum [Chelcherâgh, 1955]; Marble [Marmar, 191961]; Resurrection [Rastâkhiz, 1971]; A Line of Speed and Fire [Khatti ze Sor'at va Atash, 1980, a collection of modern ghazals]; Arzhan Plain [Dasht-e Arzhan, 1983]; Paper Dress [Kâghazin Jâmeh, USA, 1992]; A Windowful of Freedom [Yek Daricheh Âzâdi, 1995].

Hassan Honarmandi, b. 1928, Sâri, Mâzandarân.
Poetical Works: Angst [Harâs, 1969]. Other works: *From Romanticism to Surrealism* [a study of one hundred years of French poetry, 1963] and translations, particularly of André Gide.

Hushang Ebtehâj, better known by his pen name, "H. E. Sâyeh"; b. 1828, Rasht, northern province of Gilan. He was a member of the Communist Party; left Iran a few years after the Islamic Revolution, and lives in Europe.

Poetical Works: The First Songs [Nokhostin Naghmehâ, 1949]; Mirage [Sarâb, 1949]; Foredawn [Shabgir, 1953]; The Earth [Zamin, 1955]; Pages from the Longest Night [Chand Barg az Yaldâ, 1965; *Yaldâ, a Syriac word, meaning "birth", refers to Jesus Christ's day of birth, which is said to have happened on the winter solstice, the longest night of the year. For the Persians "Yaldâ" is the name given to the night of the winter solstice, and for the poet is, I think, a metaphor for the long years of repression in Iran*]; The Memorial of The Cedar's Blood [Yâdgâr-e Khun-e Sarv, 1981]; and three books of ghazals in classical style.

Sohrâb Sepehri, b. 1928, Kashan; d. Tehran, 1980.   He was also a modernist painter, influenced by the European, as well as Japanese art.

Poetical Works: The Death of Colour [Marg-e Rang, 1949]; The Life of Dreams [Zendegi-ye Khâbhâ, 1951]; Avalanche of the Sun [Âvâr-e Âftâb, 1964]; The East of Sorrow [Shargh-e Anduh, 1964]; The Footsteps of Water [Sedâ-ye Pâ-ye Âb, a long poem, 1968]; Traveller [Mosâfer, 1969, a long poem]; The Green Mass [Hajm-e Sabz, 1970]; We Nothing, We A Glance [Mâ Hich, Mâ Negâh, 1980].

Mehdi Akhavân Sâless, also known by his pen name, "M. Omid", b. 1928, Mashad, Khorasan Province; d. 1990, Tehran.

Poetical Works: Organ [Arghanun, 1954, poems in classical forms, mostly ghazal and ghasideh]; Winter [Zemestân, 1956]; The Ending of the Book of Kings [Akher-e Shâhnâmeh, 1959]; From This Avestâ [Az In Avestâ,

1965]; Hell, but Cold [Duzakh, Ammâ Sard, 1978]; Hunt [Shekâr, 1966, a long narrative poem]; Autumn in Prison [Pâ'iz dar Zendân, 1971]; Life Says: But Still One Must Live, Live, Live [Zendegi Miguyad : Ammâ Bâz Bâyad Zist, Bâyad Zist, Bâyad Zist, 1979, a long narrative poem]; O My Ancient Homeland, I love You [To râ, Ey Kohan Bum-o Bar, Dust Dâram, 1989, poems in classical forms]. Other works include *Heresies and Innovations of Nimâ Yushij* [Bed'athâ va Badâye'-e Nimâ Yushij,1979], other essays on modern poetry and two tales for children.

Nâder Nâderpur, b. 1929, Tehran. He left Iran in 1980 and, after living for some time in France, he went to the USA.

Poetical Works: Eyes and Hands [Chashmhâ va Dasthâ, 1954]; The Daughter of the Goblet [Dokhtar-e Jâm, 1955]; The Poetry of Grapes [She'r-e Angur, 1958]; The Kohl of the Sun [Sormeh-ye Khorshid,1960]; Not Plants and Stone, but Fire [Giyâh va Sang na, Âtash, 1978]; From the Sublime to the Ridiculous [Az Âsmân tâ Rismân, 1979]; The Last Supper [Shâm-e Bâz-pasin, 1979]; The False Dawn [Sobh-e Dorughin, Paris, 1982]; Blood and Ashes [Khun va Khâkestar, Los Angeles, 1989].

Manuchehr Âtashi, b. 1931 Bushehr.

Poetical Works: A New Song [Âhang-e Digar, 1964]; The Song of the Earth [Âvâz-e Khâk, 1972]; Meeting at the Dawn [Didâr dar Falagh, 1974]; In Praise of the Red Rose [Vasf-e Gol-e Suri, 1991]; Wheat and Cherries [Gandom va Gilâs, 1991]. He has also written many essays and reviews in literary magazines and periodicals.

Yadollâh Royâ'i, b. 1932 Dâmghân. He left Iran in 1975 and has been living in France ever since.

Poetical Works: On the Empty Roads [Bar Jâddehâ-ye Tohi, 1961]; Seamarks [She'rhâ-ye Daryâ'i, 1967]; Songs of Melancholy [Deltangihâ, 1968]; Of I Love You [Az Dustat Dâram, 1968]; Labial Verses [Lab-rikhtehâ, 1990]. Other works include critical essays and a Persian translation of Paul Valery's *Le Jeune Parque*.

Farrokh Tamimi, b. 1933, Nishabur, Khorasan Province.

Poetical Works: The Pure Land [Sarzamin-e Pâk, 1962]; Tired of the Dullness of Repetition [Khasteh az Birangi-ye Tekrâr, 1965]; Meeting [Didâr, 1971]; Silver and Coral [Sim va Marjân, 1973]; Embrace [Âghush, 1976]; From the Land of Mirrors and Stones [Az Sarzamin-e Âyeneh va Sang, 1977].

Bahman Forsi, b. 1933, Tehran. He is better known for his short stories and plays. He lives in London and is also a painter.

Poetical Works: Coloured by Nature [Khod-rang, London,1993]; Sound in the Hollow [Âvâ dar Kâvâk, London, 1993]; Skin and Bones [Yek Pust, Yek Ostokhân, a collection of short poems, London, 1994]. Other works include numerous plays, short stories, sketches, memoirs and a story for children.

Mahmud Mosharraf Âzâd Tehrâni, better known by his pen name, "M. Âzâd", b. 1933, Tehran.

Poetical Works: The Kingdom of Night [Diyâr-e Shab, 1954]; The Long Ode of the Wind [Ghasideh-ye Boland-e Bâd, 1966]; The Mirrors Are

Empty [Ayenehâ Tohi'st, 1967]; Spring Calving of the Deer [Bahâr-Zâ'i-ye Ahu, 1969]; Dawn with Me [Bâ Man Tolu' Kon, 1971]. He has also written several books of stories for children in prose and verse.

Forugh Farrokhzâd, b. 1933, Tehran; d. 1967,Tehran.

Poetical Works: Captive [Asir, 1955]; The Wall [Divâr, 1957]; Rebellion [Osyân, 1958]; Born Again [Tvallodi Digar, 1964]; Let Us Believe in the Beginning of the Cold Season [Imân Biyâvarim beh Âghâz-e Fasl-e Sard, 1975, published posthumously]. Other works include a documentary film about a colony of lepers in Azarbaijan Province.

Mahmud Kiânush, b. Mashad, Khorasan Province, 1934. He has been living in London since 1975.

Poetical Works: The Blossom of Astonishment [Shokufeh-ye Heyrat, 1964]; Nightland [Shabestân, a long poem, 1960]; The Herald of the Dawn [Shabâviz, a long poem, 1965]; Simple and Sad [Sâdeh va Ghamnâk, 1962]; The Moon and the Fish in the Stream of the Wind [Mâh-o Mâhi dar Chashmeh-ye Bâd, 1968]; Through the Widow of Taj-Mahal [Az Panjereh-ye Taj-Mahal, poems in prose, under a pseudonym Pradip Uma Shankar, 1971]; The Weary Waters [Abhâ-ye Khasteh, 1970]; Wood-lice, Weeds and Crows [Khar-khâkihâ, Yonjehâ va Kalâghhâ, 1973]; I Am the People [Man Mardom Hastam, a long narrative poem, London, 1978]; An Ode for Everybody [Ghasideh'i Barâye Hameh, a long poem, written in Tehran in 1970, published in Washington in 1987]; Where Is That Voice? [Kojâ'st An Sedâ?, a long poem, 1992]. He has also written poems for children and young adults, novels and short stories including several books of stories for children, critical works and translations of John Steinbeck, D.H. Lawrence, Samuel Beckett and others.

Touraj Rahnamâ, b. 1937, Ahvâz, Khuzestan Province. He is a lecturer of German literature in Tehran University, and has published several books of his German Translations of Persian contemporary fiction and poetry.

Poetical Works: Oyster and the Tale of Its Loneliness [Sadaf va Ghesseh-ye Tanhâ'i-ye U, 1971]; To the Land of Swallows, To the Moon [Tâ Sarzamin-e Chelchelehâ, tâ Mâh, 1975]; In the Silence of the Rose [Dar Sokut-e Gol-e Sorkh].

Shâdâb Vajdi, b. 1937, Shirâz. She has been living in London since 1971, and currently teaches Persian language and literature at the School of Oriental and African Studies, London.

Poetical Works: The Bend of the Alley [Kham-e Hucheh, 1960]; A Song for Little Hands [Sorudi Barâye Dasthâ'i Huchek, 1968]; To the Memory of the Thirst of Southern Mountain Slopes [Beh Yâd-e Teshnegi-ye Kuhpâyehâ-ye Janub, London, 1982]; Another Day [Yek Ruz-e Digar, 1992]; Close Circuit, [Selected Poems, translated from the Persian by Lotfali Khonji, London, 1990]; Under Rainfall [Zir-e Bârân, U.S.A., 1995].

Meymanat Mirsâdeghi, also known by her pen name, "Âzâdeh", b. 1937, Estahbânât, Fârs Province.

Poetical Works: The Wakefulness of the Streams [Bidâri-ye Juybârân, 1968]; With Waters and Mirrors [Bâ Âbhâ va Âyenehâ, 1977]; Sunny Souls [Jânhâ-ye Âftâbi, 1992]. Other works include *Terminology of Poetical Art* [Vâzheh-nâmeh-ye Honar-e Shâeri, 1994].

Tâhereh Saffârzâdeh, b. 1938, Sirjan, Kerman Province.

Poetical Works: The Passage of Moonlight [Rahgozar-e Mahtâb, 1964]; Red Parasol [Chatr-e Sorkh, poems written in English, published in the USA, by the University of Iowa, 1970]; The Echo in the Delta [Tanin dar Deltâ, 1972]; The Dam and the Arms [Sadd va Bâzovân, 1973]; The Fifth Journey [Safar-e Panjom, 1978.]; Movement and Yesterday [Harekat va Diruz, 1979]; Allegiance With Wakefulness [Bey'at Bâ Bidâri, 1980]; Meeting in the Morning [Didâr dar Sobh, 1988]. Other works include a novel.

Esmâ'il Kho'i, b. 1938, Mashad, Khorasan Province. He left Iran in 1984, and has been living in London ever since.

Poetical Works: Restless [Bitâb, 1956]; On the Steed of the Earth [Bar Kheng-e Râhvâr-e Zamin, 1967]; On the Roof of the Whirlwind [Bar Bâm-e Gerdbâd, 1970]; Than the Sound of the Words of Love [Az Sedâ-ye Sokhân-e Eshgh, 1970]; Of Those Seafarers [Z'An Rahrovân-e Daryâ, 1970]; Beyond the Night of These People [Farâtar az Shab-e Aknuniyân, 1971]; On the Shores of Sitting and Being [Bar Sâhel-e Neshastan va Hastan, 1973]; We, the Beings [Mâ Budegân, 1979]; The Wakeful's Nightmare of Bloodbath [Kâbus-e Khunsereshteh-ye Bidârân, London, 1984]; Untimely [Dar Nabehangâm, London, 1985]; Because the Earth Is the Earth [Zirâ Zamin Zamin Ast, London, 1985]; Send Me A Piece of the Blue Sky [Yek Tekkeh'am Âsmân-e Âbi Beferest, quatrains, London, 1995]. He has also published an interview and essays on the writing of poetry.

Mansur Owji, b. Shirâz, Fârs Province, 1939.

Poetical Works: The Garden of Night [Bâgh-e Shab, 1965]; The Exhausted City [Shahr-e Khasteh, 1968]; Sleep and Tree [Khâb va Derakht,

1970]; The Loneliness of the Earth [Tanhâ'i-ye Zamin, 1970]; This Is Susan Who Sings [In Susan Ast Keh Mikhânad, 1971]; The Voice of Eternity [Sedâ-ye Hamisheh, 1978]; Poems As Short As Life [She'rhâ'i beh Kutâhi-ye Omr, 1979]; Short Like A Sigh [Kutâh Mesl-e Ah, 1989].

Ne'mat Mirzâzâdeh, better known by his pen name, "M. Âzarm", b. 1939, Mashad, Khorasan Province. About two years after the 1979 Revolution, disillusioned with the Islamic regime, he left Iran, and currently lives in France.

Poetical Works: Message [Payâm, a long ghasideh in praise of Mohammad and his mission, 1968]; Awakening Knock [Sahuri, 1970]; Watchman [Gozarbân, 1979]; Flight in Storm [Parvâz dar Tufân, 1979]; Seraph's Trumpet [Sur-e Esrâfil, 1979]; Wrath Flower [Gol-khashm, 1979]; Blood Flower [Gol-khun, 1981]; With Desire for My Homeland [Be Havâ-ye Mihan, 1982].

Mohammad-Rezâ Shafi'i Kadkani, also known by his pen name, "M. Sereshk", b. 1939, Mashad, Khorasan Province. He is a professor of Persian literature in Tehran University.

Poetical Works: The Murmurs [Zemzemehâ, 1965]; Hushed Songs of Night [Shabkhâni, 1965]; In the Language of the Leaves [Az Zabân-e Barg, 1968]; In the Garden-paths of Nishâbur [Dar Kuch-bâghhâ-ye Nishâbur, 1971]; Like Trees in A Rainy Night [Mesl-e Derakht dar Shab-e Bârân, 1977]; The Sweet Smell from the Muliyân River [Bu-ye Ju-ye Muliyân, 1978]; Of Being and Singing [Az Budan va Sorudan, 1979]. His other works include several critical studies of Persian poetry, a study of the progressive movements in the Arabic poetry in the twentieth century and translations from modern Arabic poetry.

Mohammad-Ali Sepânlu, b. 1940, Tehran.
Poetical Works: Ah, Desert! [Ah, Biyâbân!, 1963]; The Earth [Khâk,

a long poem, 1965]; The Showers [Ragbârhâ, 1967]; The Pavements [Piyâdeh-rwohâ, a long poem, 1968]; The Absent Sindbad [Sendbâd-e Ghâyeb, 1973]; Attack [Hojum, 1977]; I take the Pulse of My Country [Nabz-e Vatanam râ Migiram, 1978]; The Lady of Time [Khânom-e Zamân, London,1987]. Other works include a collection of short stories, essays, and a short history of literary criticism in Iran.

from The Pavements   195

Ahmad-Rezâ Ahmadi, b. 1940, Kerman.
Poetical Works: Sketch [Tarh, 1962]; A Glass Newspaper [Ruz-nâmeh-ye Shisheh'i, 1964]; The Happy Time of Calamities [Vaght-e Khub-e Masâ'eb, 1968]; I Only Wept the Whiteness of the Horse [Man Faghat Sefidi-ye Asb râ Geristam, 1971]; We Are on the Earth [Mâ Ruye Zamin Hastim, 1973]; A Thousand Steps Are Left to the Sea [Hezâr Pelleh beh Daryâ Mândeh Ast,1985]; The Rhyme Is Lost in the Wind [Ghâfiyeh dar Bâd Gom Shod, 1990]. Other works include screenplays and several books of stories for children.

Poem Nine: For Spring   197

Esmâ'il Nuri-Alâ, also known by his pen name "E. N. Payâm", b. 1943, Tehran. He is a journalist and the co-editor of a Persian literary periodical called "Puyeshgarân". After the 1979 Revolution he left Iran, and lived in London until 1994, when he moved to the USA.
Poetical Works: Tales For Mâmâ Jimjim [Ghessehâ'i Barâye Mâmmâ Jimjim, 1962]; The Rooms With Closed Doors [Otâghhâ-ye Dar-basteh, 1965]; With the People of the Night [Bâ Mardom-e Shab, 1969]; The Prohibited Land [Sarzamin-e Mamnu', 1978]; Still the Mount Damâvand [Hanuz Damâvand, London, 1988]; Three Steps To Glory [Seh Pelleh tâ Shokuh,1991; Shokuh, which means glory, is the name of his second wife who is a novelist and short story writer]. He has also written books about the theory and practice of poetry.

Their Expectation   200

Minâ Asadi, b. 1943, Sâri, Mâzandarân Province. She lives in Sweden.
Poetical Works: Minâ's Present [Armaghân-e Minâ, 19??]; Who Is Throwing Stones? [Cheh Kasi Sang Mi-andazad?, 1971]; Of Love Nothing Is Left with the World [Az Eshgh bâ Jahân Chizi Namândeh Ast, 1987, London, 1987]; A Ring to Me Is Bondage [Man beh Angoshtar Mi-guyam

Band, London, 1988]; Work Report [Kârnâmeh, London, 1988]. She has also published studies of Iranian children living in Sweden, of immigrants and racism, and of prostitution in Iran.

Zhilâ Mosâ'ed, b. 1948, Tehran. She lives in Sweden.

Poetical Works: The Brisk Gazelles of Memories [Ghazâlân-e Châlâk-e Khâtereh, 1985]; Reclining in the Palanquin of Sorrow [Yaleh bar Kajâveh-ye Anduh, Sweden, 1989]; Those Who Hide the Fire [Penhân-konandegân-e Âtash, Germany, 1991]; The Moon and That Eternal Bull [Mâh va Ân Gâv-e Azali, Sweden, 1993]. Her other works include a novel.

Ali-Rezâ Nurizâdeh, b. 1949, Tehran. He is a journalist and lives in London.

Poetical Works: Through the Window [Az Posht-e Shisheh, 1968]; The Bleeding Box Trees [Shemshâdhâ-ye Khunin, 1970]; Alpha, Lamtha, Mi [Alef, Lâm, Mim, 1971 — these letters are the title of one of the chapters of Koran]; The One-thousand-and-first Night [Shab-e Hezâr-o Yekom, London, 1988]; My Country, Light and Water and Fragrance and Honey [Vatanam, Nur va Âb va Atr va Asal, London and Los Angeles, 1994]. He has also written a story about the 1979 Revolution in Iran, based on his memories.

Mirzâ. Âghâ Askari, also known by his pen name "Mâni", b. 1950, Asadâbâd, Hamadân. He left Iran in 1983 and lives in Germany.

Poetical Works: Tomorrow Is the First Day of the World [Fardâ Avvalin Ruz-e Donyâ'st, 1975]; I Have Relations with Waters [Man bâ Âbhâ Râbeteh Dâram, 1976]; The Songs of Peace [Tarâneha-ye Solh, 1982]; The Songs of the Republic [Âvâzhâ-ye Jomhuri, 1982]; The Land of Bitterness [Dar Sarzamin-e Talkh, Germany, 1987]; Moon in the Mirror [Mâh dar Âyeneh, Germany, 1988]; Flight in Storm [Parvâz dar Tufân, Germany, 1989]; Love, the Last Salvation [Eshgh, Vâpasin Rastgâri, Germany, 1991]; Under the Tree of Words [Zir-e Derakht-e Vâzheh, Germany, 1993]. Other works include literary criticism and several stories and plays for children.

Hamid-Rezâ Rahimi, b. 1950, Kermânshâh. He is also a calligrapher. *Poetical Works:*   Moments Are Honest [Lahzehâ Sâdeghand, 1971]; Closed, Empty Space [Fazâ-ye Khâli-ye Masdud, 1979]; From Far Away, in Exile [Az Dur-dast-e Tab'id, Germany, 1986]; Mural Murmurs [Zemzemehâ-ye Divari, Germany, 1986]; The Winter Solstice [Yaldâ, bilingual, German and Persian, Germany, 1989]; Shower in Sunshine [Ragbâr dar Âftâb, Germany, 1989]; A Quarter to Destruction [Yek Rob' beh Virâni, Germany, 1991]. Other works include the life and works of Farrokhi Yazdi, a poet who died in prison in 1939.

Asadollâh Sha'bâni, b. 1958, Hamadân.   He is better known as a children's poet and writer, and so far has published about forty books of poems and stories for children and young adult. A collection of his poems for adults was published in 1989, entitled "Nightly Wanderings" [Parsehâ-ye Shabâneh].

Behruz Eftekhâri, b. 1966, Tehran.   His first book of poems was published in 1991, entitled "The Sound of Breaking Silence" [Sedâ-ye Shekastan-e Sokut].

Nimâ Yushij
(1895—1969)

COLD ASHES

From nights long gone
Round a handful of cold ashes,
Once a small fire,
A few stones are still left
On a peaceful path through the forest.

Like the woeful trace of an image
In the dust of my thoughts,
Every line of it a story of long sufferings.

My sweet day that was at peace with me,
Has changed to some sinister image,
Something cold and solid like a stone;

The breath of the autumn of my life,
An allusion to my fading spring :
Round a handful of cold ashes,
Once a small fire,
A few stones are still left
On a peaceful path through the forest
From nights long gone.

O PEOPLE!

O people who are sitting, cheerful and laughing,
          on the shore,
Someone is losing his life in the sea;
Someone is struggling in the rough, dark
          and formidable sea.
Just when you are intoxicated with the thought
          of conquering your enemies;
When you are deluding yourselves

that by helping one poor man you are building
        prosperity for all;
When you are girding up your loins
        for some endeavour;
Of what other concerns of yours should I speak?
Yes, all this while someone's life
        is being needlessly sacrificed in the sea.

O people who have an exhilarating time on the shore:
Your tables bountiful, your bodies well clothed,
Someone in the sea is calling you for help,
He is buffeting the heavy waves
        with his exhausted hands;
He is gasping for breath,
        his eyes bulging out of their sockets in terror;
Water has filled his inside in the dark deep,
And in his growing distress
Out of the water he thrusts
Now his head, now his feet,
O people!

He tries not to lose sight
        of this old world from far away,
And with the hope of some help he cries out;
O people, who are enjoying the view
        from the peaceful shore!

Waves rush in, pounding on the silent shore,
        toppling like drunken men,
        lying sprawled out, unconscious,
And then, roaring they retreat into the sea.
Again the same cry comes from far away:
"O people ..."

And the wind has a more tormenting sound
And the cry of the man in the sea
        is spreading out in the sound of the wind,
And from the midst of the water,
        close and distant,
Again this cry echoes:
"O people ..."

MY HEART OF STEEL

Leave me alone,
— Me, the babbler —
And do not take away my horse,
My saddle-cover and my provision,
Because a restive thought
Has drawn me out of my house.

I have returned from a land
Where no happiness is found.
I have seen lands
Which are the bases of vicious rebels
Who occupy themselves with massacres;
Lands, with spring planted in every corner,
Not flowers, but the wounds of men slain.

On my way, I thought in vain
That any traveller could pass
Through this desert of death
If he had a heart of steel
And could nonchalantly observe good and evil,
Taking all problems easily,
Knowing this world
As the place of hatred and murder,
The place of destruction and wretchedness.

But now I see that my return,
With all the wisdom I put to use,
Has been to the same desert of death,
And the horrible nightmares which have been
My memories from my journey
Are still alive before my eyes,
Burning my existence
In their annihilating fire.

For me, a ruined man of travel,
There is not a moment of time to stay;
Now I am more plundered than anyone else;
I have lost whatever I had,

My heart of steel is no longer with me;
I was nothing but my heart,
And now I see
That my heart of steel is left behind on the way;
There is no doubt
That my heart has been thrown
By those malicious people
Into the arms of a spring
Whose flowers, as I said,
Are of blood and wounds.
And now I am thinking that my heart of steel
Would change,
Rusting in the blood of my brothers
So innocently, so unjustly slain.

SNOW

Yellows have not turned red without reason;
Nor has red coloured the walls by chance.
Morning has emerged from behind the Azâ Mountain, [1]
But Mount Vâznâ [2] is not visible.
The pale whiteness of a snow
That can only disturb everything,
Has blurred the windowpanes.

Vâznâ is not visible;
My heart is bitterly heavy
Because of this gloomy guest-killer of a guesthouse
That incites a bunch of strangers,
A bunch of sleepy, ignorant blunderers,
To cut each other's throats.

[1]   *Azâkuh, a mountain range in Mâzandarân, one of the northern provinces of Iran, where the village of Yush, the poet's birthplace, is situated.*

[2]   *Vâznâ is a mountain near Yush.*

IT IS NIGHT

It is night,
A night of deep darkness.
On a branch of the old fig tree
      a frog croaks without cease,
Predicting a storm, a deluge,
      and I am drowned in fear.

It is night,
And with night the world seems
      like a corpse in the grave;
And in fear I say to myself:
"What if torrential rain falls everywhere?
"What if the rain does not stop
      until the earth sinks into the water
      like a small boat?"

In this night of awful darkness
Who can say in what state we will be
      when dawn breaks?
Will the morning light make
      the frightening face of the storm
      disappear?

A MOTH FROM THE NEARBY SHORE

Chook ... chook ... a moth from the nearby shore
Has lost its way in the dark night
And it knocks on my window incessantly.

O the moth from the nearby shore,
What is the purpose of your struggle?
What do you want in my room?

The moth from the nearby shore,
      says to me in a peculiar utterance:
"How flooded with light is your room!

I beg of you, let me in!
So tired I am of the night!"

The moth from the nearby shore
        must be very ignorant to think
That everyone can follow
        whatever direction they choose;
That every way may lead
        to safety and comfort;
Or that any light is surely a way
        out of darkness.

Chook ... chook ...
        then why is that on such a night
Which breeds.pain and sorrow,
No one wants to choose
        my way to follow?

Fereydun Tavallali
(1919—1985)

WRETCHEDNESS

My soul is bored of the repetition
        of days and nights,
My heart tired, my problems unsolved;
But still that bitter, black hope,
Like a broken dagger,
        remains in my breast.

In the demon-land of my existence
There is a life-giving,
        pain-fostering secret
        burning;
I keep myself alive by concealing
        that secret
With a thousand flaming wounds.

My lips are sealed like some old scar
Lest this secret should devour me again;
I show a sullen face lest the inquisitive
Should fall on me
        with their powerful resentment.

The sunshine finds no way
        through my solitude,
It is all darkness, cold and lostness;
I am sick of the dusk at sunset
And of light at the break of dawn.

I am living death in my sorrows,
Though in company of the living
        I share their noisy joys;
Beware of my wretchedness, beware!
I am a man who makes love
        with the corpse of his dead hope.

Shahnâz A'lâmi
(b. 1921)

MAGIC SUITCASE

I took with me a suitcase,
    light, very light;
Two or three sets of baby clothes,
A white georgette dress,
An indistinct photograph of my mother,
    wearing a headdress,
And a complete list of traditional things
    for the Noe-Rooz's celebrations, [3]
Lest a single thing should be forgotten;
These were what I had,
    or rather, people thought I had,
    in my suitcase
With which I left the land
    of the generous sun.
My suitcase was,
    or rather, people thought it was,
    very, very light;
But what a big mistake!
You must have seen the shows
    of professional magicians;
They put their fingers
    up their sleeves,
And take out whatever you may name:
Birds, rabbits, kerchiefs of all colours,
Sometimes a crystal jug,
Sometimes a piece of stone,
Fire, water, soil,
Flowers, thorns and many other things;
So was my empty magic suitcase.

[3]   *Noe-Rooz, or Now Ruz, the Persian New Year's Day (21 March in the Western calendar) is followed by twelve days of celebrations and visiting relatives and friends.*

Now it has been almost a lifetime
That from inside the same suitcase
I have been taking out anything I want:
Wonderful springs of Isfahân
And its exhilarating groves
      in the outskirts;
The colourful autumn of Shirâz
And the fragrance of its orange trees;
The ancient ruins of Persepolis; [4]
The Baghestân Mountain
      with its historical inscriptions;
The Palace of Princess Shirin;
The poor village of Cham in Nâ'in; [5]
The tattered dress of Fâtima,
      a peasant little girl,
And a flock of other children like her,
Who are all in the same suitcase.

I take them out;
I sit and talk with them;
I live with them;
And the moment someone appears,
They all run back into the suitcase,
The very suitcase which people think
      must be very light
      and almost empty.

When I make my will
I will ask for my suitcase
      to be buried with me.

[4]   *Persepolis was the ceremonial capital of Darius, Xerxes and other kings of the Archaemenid period. Baghestân Mountain, near Kermânshâh in western Iran, has on its face a bas-relief depicting Darius I, with captive chiefs and a record of his reign. In the same province was the palace of Shirin, an Armenian princess who is said to have been the wife of Khosrow Parviz (521—628), one of the greatest kings of the Sassanid period.*

[5]   *Cham is a village near the town of Nâ' in, famous for its carpets.*

No doubt they will say:
"Her life was madness;
And her will is foolish!
What sort of will is that!
Who needs a suitcase
in the other world?"

Let them say whatever they like;
After all,
who does know the secret
of the professional magician of love?
Is it not true that *love*
is the astrolabe of God's mysteries? [6]

[6] *The words in italics are part of a famous couplet from the "Masnavi" of Jalâl-od-Din Rumi, one of the greatest Persian mystic or Sufi poets, who is also known as Mowlavi. He lived a good part of his life in Konya in Turkey, where his tomb is a shrine for a dervish sect known as "Mowlaviyyeh".*

Zhâleh Esfahâni
(b. 1921)

FOREST AND RIVER

"I wish I were like you,"
Said the forest
      to the roaring river,
"Always travelling,
      always sightseeing;
Rushing towards the pure domain
      of the sea,
The kingdom of water;
Water,
The passionate, vigorous spirit
      of life,
The liquid turquoise of light
With eternal flow ...

"But what am I?
Only a captive,
      chained to the earth.
In silence I grow old,
In silence I wither and die,
And before long
      nothing will remain of me
But a handful of ashes."

"O forest, half-asleep, half-awake,"
Cried the river,
"I wish I were you,
Enjoying a seclusion
      of living emerald,
And illuminated by moonlit nights;
Being a mirror
      reflecting the beauties
      of Spring;
A shaded rendezvous for lovers.

"Your destiny, a new life
            every year;
My life, running away from myself
            all the time;
Running, running, running
            in bewilderment;
And what is my gain
Of all this meaningless journey?
Ah ... never having a moment of calm
            and rest!

"No one can ever know
            what the other feels;
Who does care to ask
            about a passer-by
If he really existed
Or was only a shadow?"

Now a passer-by
Aimlessly walking in the shade
Comes to ask himself,
"Who am I? a river? a forest?
Or both?
River and forest?
River and forest!"

THE MIRROR OF OLD FAITHS

In the mirror of Faith,
            now bright, now dark,
How mystical is the image
            of our Beauty, the Truth,
            in her dance of Love!
O enlightening Thought
Make me a prism of light
            amid the shadows;
Crush my ore,
            melt me,
            and mould me

into a crystal cup,
And let me be filled to the brim
        with the pure wine of awakening,
Out of the veil of dreamy,
        intoxicating illusions.

It is a fatal avalanche
Rushing down the moutainside,
Pulling us along to our doom;
And yet you may think
        it is only imagination!

Man flies higher and higher
Across the realms of space;
And I,
        though sitting in a dull corner,
Have a heart burning with desire
        for a flight above and beyond
        all the horizons.

The old clothes of the past
        do not suit me any more,
For the designer of Time
        introduces new fashions everyday.

The past belonged to another world
        where I was also another person;
And today the world is a different one;
The horizon is not only grey sometimes
        and sometimes red or blue;
It bears thousands and thousands of colours,
        and mysteries,
Which must be seen
        in the new mirror of a new faith.

WHEN YOU SMILE

When you smile,
      with you smiles the rose of the sun.
When you smile,
The desert blooms with tulips and daffodils,
And golden canaries begin to sing.
When you smile,
      everything,
      even doors and walls begin to dance.
When you smile,
      my sorrows quietly sleep
And my hopes awake.

If sometimes you see me weeping
      do not worry,
Because a mother's fate is to cry,
      sometimes with sorrow,
      sometimes with joy:
When her son falls ill,
When her son is hurt by someone,
Or when others,
      relatives or strangers,
      are hurt by her son;
When her son comes home too late
      at night;
When her son takes a bride
And nests on a new tree;
At all these times
      a mother cries with sorrow
      or with joy ...

When you smile,
      the ocean swells with waves of pearls;
When you smile,
      with you smiles the rose of the sun.

Manucher Sheybâni
(1923—1991)

SLAVE-GIRL

O maiden of the land of fairy tales,
No one pays a farthing
For the pearls of your tears
In the markets of the East.

The perfume and silk merchants,
In whose hands apple blossoms
    turn into chains,
Will take you as a slave-girl,
But they will display you as the jewel
    in the crown of their shops;
A plaything for the orgies of the nobles,
Those tricksters who turn the soft air
    into bars of gold.

They are so busy watching
    the rapid growth of figures
That they have no time
    for turning their eyes
To cast a glance
    at the land of beauties
Across the horizon
    of your transparent body.
In the tumultuous boom
    of the Oriental markets
The delightful rhythm of your gait
Will be broken by the march
    of profit and loss.

O chariot of glass and crystal,
To where can you go
By taking this perilous, stony path?
The green road of Spring
    is open to you

Up to the gates of the rainbow.
But you,
        broken and helpless,
Resemble the bewildered eyes
        of a lost star.
O maiden of the Lost Paradise,
I see paradise in the silky wheatfields
        of your eyelashes.

O wanderer in the deserts of illusion,
Can you not see the wicked wizard
        in front of you,
Who drags you, like a slave-girl,
        wherever he likes,
With his promises of colourful mirages,
With the magic dance of empty images?

O the wandering maiden
        of uncharted deserts,
O the fragrance of the caravans
        of silk and perfume,
Be only mine,
And let your mercury fingers
Play the harp for my songs
        of thousandfold melodies; .
Songs which make and raise high
        the banner of love
Up to the farthest galaxies,
Because the merchants
        in the markets of the East
Will not give a farthing
For the pearls of your tears.

Ahmad Shâmlu [A. Bâmdâd]
(b. 1925)

DROP OF THE CURTAIN

Lovers went away in disgrace,
Ashamed before Songs
Because they sang them
    at an inappropriate time.

And the streets
Are left empty of the murmur
    of voices
And the sound of steps.

Soldiers went away stricken,
Exhausted,
    riding on skeletal horses,
Faded rags of an overthrown pride
Hanging from their spears!

What is the good of shouting your pride
    to stars,
When each particle of the dust
    in the accursed road curses you!

What is the good of gardens and trees
    to you,
Who have spoken to jasmines
With the tongue of scythes!

Plants refuse to grow in earth
Where you have once trodden,
Because you cannot believe
    in the piety of Soil and Water.
Alas! the history of our lives
Was nothing but the untruthful war songs
    of your soldiers,
Whose triumph was the conquest
    of the Harlots' Fortress.

Wait and see what the curse of the night
Will make you suffer,
Because the mothers in black,
Who mourn for the most beautiful sons
        of the Sun and the Wind,
Have yet to raise their heads
From their prayer mats!

THE HOUR OF EXECUTION

A key turned in the keyhole.
A smile quivered on the man's lips
Like the dance of sunlight
Reflected by water on the ceiling.

A key turned in the keyhole.

Outside
The pleasant colour of the dawn
Seemed like a lost note
Searching for its home,
Hovering along the holes of a flute.

A key turned in the keyhole,
A smile danced on the man's lips,
Like the dance of sunlight
Reflected on the ceiling.

A key turned in the keyhole.

ANOTHER TORMENT

The dagger of evil
        would have not pierced my heart
If there was a little goodness
        in your hearts;
The stroking hands

would have not been stained
with blood
If your fingernails were not tempered
with the poison of enmity.

Otherwise why do your kisses make my lips bleed?
Why do smiles fill my eyes with tears?
Why does water from pure springs
turn into poison?
Why does the bush of love gives blossoms of anger?

What can I say to people,
When they ask me
about this painful, unhealable wound?
Perhaps I should say nothing,
Otherwise no one will ever submit his heart
to love again.

RELIEF

The absolute darkness of being blind,
The deadly feeling of being forlorn.

"What time is it?"
you ask yourself.
"What day? what month of what year?
of what century?
of what calendar?
of what planet?"

Suddenly a single cough
from beside you:
Ah, a relieving perception
of having someone
with whom to share the light.

LOOK!

1

The year of evil,
The year of *simoom*, [7]
The year of tears,
The year of doubt.
The year of long days,
    and brief endurance,
The year when pride was forced to beg.
The year of wickedness,
    of pain,
    of mourning;
The year of Puri's tears,
The year of Mortazâ's blood,
The leap year.

2

Life is not a snare;
Love is not a snare;
Even death is not a snare,
Because our lost comrades are free,
They are free and pure.

3

I found my love in an evil year;
Who says
    "Don't despair!"
I found my hope in despair;
I found the moonlight in darkness;

[7] *The simoom is a hot, dry, and violent wind, laden with dust from the desert, and used by many modern Persian poets as a metaphor for disastrous historical events, like the Shah's coup d'état in 1953, when the Mossadeq government was overthrown and many members of the Tudeh (Communist) party were executed or imprisoned. Mortazâ (Keyvân) was among the executed: Puri is the name of his wife.*

I found my love in an evil year.
And when I was reduced to ashes,
    I began to flame.

Life bore me a resentment;
I smiled at life.
Earth showed enmity against me;
I lay down on earth,
Because life is not darkness,
Because earth is good.

I was bad, but I was not evil;
I escaped evil
        and the world cursed me,
        and the evil year arrived:
The year of Puri's tears,
The year of Mortazâ's blood,
The year of darkness.
And I found my star,
I found goodness,
I reached goodness
And blossomed.

You are good
And this is the whole confession.
I have spoken the truth
        and I have wept,
But this time I speak the truth
        and smile,
Because my last tears
        were my first smiles.

4

You are good
And I was not evil;
I came to know you,
        I found you,
        I understood you,
        and all my words became poetry,
        became light.
My pains became poetry, all burdens

became poetry, grass became poetry,
enmity became poetry,
And all poems became goodness;
The sky sang its song,
birds sang their songs,
water sang its song.
I said to you:
"Be my little sparrow
So that in your springtime
I may become a tree
in full blossom."
And snow melted,
blossoms danced,
and the sun rose.
I looked at all good things
and changed;
I looked at good things
Because you are good
and this is the whole confession,
the greatest of all confessions.
I looked at confessions,
The evil year departed
and I became alive again;
You smiled and I stood up.

5

I want to be good,
I want to be "YOU"
and this is why
I say the truth.

Look!
Stay with me.

THE FIFTH SONG

This is the grey fragrance of the air,
      heralding the morning.
The earth is pregnant with another day.
This is the white murmur;
This is the sun that will rise soon.
The stars are melting away one by one,
      and the night
Piece by piece breaks into small shadows,
Which take refuge behind anything;
And the cool breeze is felt
      like gentle strokes.

Our love is a village that, night and day,
      never sleeps;
A village where,
      even for a moment,
Power and passion of life never subside.
It is time for me to drink your teeth,
      like warm milk,
In the long draught of a kiss.

To win the touch of your hand
I am willing to climb any mountain,
To pass through any desert,
To sail across any ocean.

A day that begins so beautifully
Is not for being spent in separation from you,
(At a time when,
      along with the vanishing night,
I have given the last words
      of the tragedy of the past
      to the memoryless wind.)
You are the wind, the blossoms, the fruits,
O my all seasons!
Pass by my life like a year
And I will begin to live an eternity.

THE GARDEN OF MIRROR

With a lamp in my hand,
    and a lamp shining ahead,
I am on my way
    to fight against darkness.

The cradles of weariness
    have stopped swaying,
And in the depths a sun
    lightens the burnt-out galaxies.

The riotous cries of lightning,
When the hailstones take form
    in the restless wombs of clouds;
And the silent pain of the vine
When the baby grapes appear
    at the top of long, winding branches:

My cry was all an escape from pain,
Because, in the most horrible nights,
I have been seeking the sun
    with a hopeless prayer.

You have come from the suns,
    from the dawns.

In a void where there was neither God,
    nor fire,
I have been seeking your glances
    and your trust
    with a hopeless prayer.

A vital current
Between two deaths
In the emptiness between two solitudes:
Your trust is something like this!

Your joy is ruthless and noble,
Your breaths in my empty hands
    are songs and grass.

I rise!
A lamp in my hand, a lamp in my heart.
I polish my rusty soul.
I set a mirror opposite yours
To make your image infinite.

EPIC!

Nothing new happens at the crossroads;
There are those who go,
And those who come back,
        utterly tired;
And man
— who, without doubt,
        is an ancient, clever god —
Is selling condoms
        at the passage of Time,
Without emotion, without hope,
For only two loaves of bread.

In the street,
        a poet stops suddenly
And spontaneously writes
        these epic lines
        on the back of a cigarette packet:

"Man is God,
        this is my belief;
Whether it is a sacrilege,
        or the absolute truth,
What I have to say
        is that Man is God!"

The sudden ringing
        of some jackass of a cyclist
Startles the poet,
        and ...
... and the lead of his pencil
        breaks ...

NOCTURNE

If the Night is pointlessly beautiful
Why is it beautiful,
And for whom?
The Night and the untwisting river
        of the stars
Which coldly flows?
For the remembrance of whom
The long-haired mourners on both sides
        of the river
Are lamenting with the dreadful dirges
        of the frogs,
When dawns are riddled
With simultaneous sounds of twelve bullets?

If the Night is pointlessly beautiful,
For whom is the Night beautiful,
And why?

ÂYDÂ[8] IN THE MIRROR

Your lips, with the elegance of poetry,
Can transform the most lustful kisses
        into such modesty
That by the grace of which
        a cave-dwelling beast
Becomes human.

And your cheeks,
        with slanting hollows,
Give direction to your pride
        and to my destiny;
And I am a man who resisted
        the dread of the night,
Without being armed

[8]   *Âydâ is the name of Shâmlu's third wife.*

89

with a delivering dawn;
And proudly returned
        from the brothels of trade
With the virginity of my soul
        untouched.

No one has ever been
        more cruelly wasteful
        in killing himself
Than I have been in living my life.

And your eyes are of fire;
And your love is the victory of man
When he ventures on fighting
        against destiny;
And your bosom is a cosy, little place
        for living,
        a safe little corner for dying;
And a haven to shelter
        from the demon of the city
With its thousands of defiling fingers
Pointing to the purity of the sky.

A mountain begins its existence
        with the first rocks,
And man with his first sorrows.

There was a cruel prisoner in me
Who stood firm not to reconcile himself
To the sounds of his chains;
I began my existence
        with your first glance.

Your overwhelming dance
Makes the storms gloriously play the harp,
And the songs of your veins
Make the sun of eternity rise.

Let me rise from sleep in such a way
That everybody in the town
Would become aware of my presence.

Your hands are the spirit of peace;
Your hands are good friends
        by whose grace
        enmity can be driven
        into oblivion;
Your forehead is a high, bright mirror
In which the moon and the stars
Find their beauty surpassed.

Your bosom has caged two birds
        which restlessly sing.

No matter from what climate
        the summer comes,
It cannot make any water taste pleasant
        to my thirst.

Waiting for you to appear in the mirror,
I, who had wept all the oceans,
All my life have stared into its depths;
O fairy in human form,
Whose body is immune to all fires
        except the fire of falsehood,
Your presence is a paradise
        where I can shelter
        from the earthly hells;
An ocean that embraces me
And washes away all the sins and lies.

And the dawn awakes by your hands.

LOVE SONG

A short sojourn is life
        in the journey between sin and hell.
The sun
        rises like a curse
and the day
Is an indelible shame.

Oh!
Say something before I drown in tears.

Trees
Are the sinful ignorance of our ancestors,
And breezes
        vicious temptations.
The autumn moonlight
Is a sacrilege
        which defiles the world.

Say something;
Before I drown in tears,
        say something.

Every beautiful window
Opens to a scene of torture and agony.
Love
        is a filthy, nauseous fluid,
And the sky
        only a roof over your head,
While you sit on the earth
                weeping over your destiny.

Oh,
Say something before I drown in tears;
Say something, whatever it may be.

Springs
Gush out of coffins,
And distressed mourners
        are the honour of the world.
Do not sell innocence to the mirrors,
Because the debauchers are more in want of it.

Do not sit silent,
        for God's sake!
Before I drown in tears
        say something of Love!

IN THIS DEAD END

They smell your mouth [9]
To find out if you have told someone:
I love you!
They smell your heart!
Such a strange time it is, my dear;
And they punish Love
At thoroughfares
By flogging.
  We must hide our Love in dark closets.

In this crooked dead end of a bitter cold
They keep their fire alive
By burning our songs and poems;
Do not place your life in peril by your thoughts!
Such a strange time it is, my dear!
He who knocks on your door in the middle of the night,
His mission is to break your Lamp!
  We must hide our Lights in dark closets!

Behold! butchers are on guard at thoroughfares
With their bloodstained cleavers and chopping-boards;
Such a strange time it is, my dear!
They cut off the smiles from lips,
And the songs from throats! [9]
  We must hide our Emotions in dark closets!

They barbecue canaries
On a fire of jasmines and lilacs!
Such a strange time it is, my dear!
Intoxicated by victory,
Satan is enjoying a feast at our mourning table !
  We must hide our God in dark closets!

[9]   *In the early days of the Islamic Revolution, young men and women were sent into the streets to enforce the moral code of the shari'a or religious law, in some cases acting violently and excessively.   They "smelled the mouth" if they suspected someone of drinking alcohol, which could be followed by a lashing, and they wiped lipstick from women's mouths, sometimes even cutting the lips with a razor.*

Esmâ'il Shâhrudi [Âyandeh]
(1925—1981)

GREEN GARDEN

Tonight my breath is a savage
    in my chest,
Beating his drum
    on the cliff of fear;
Someone is knocking at the door;
It is the wind, I say to my fear,
    it is the wind;
Whoever but the wind may call upon
    an isolated tree!

Someone is knocking at the door!
And with every beat of the drum
I struggle to find a way
    out of this fright.

Someone is knocking at the door
    softer than before;
And when I want to say
    to myself again
    that it is the wind ...
Resemblance takes the softer knocks
    into the drip of rain
And sends them softly,
    through my ears,
Into the garden of my eyes,
And I find relief
    in the green garden of my eyes,
And night becomes quiet,
And the door stays undisturbed.

Fereydun Moshiri
(b. 1925)

IF THE GOBLET BREAKS

In my eyes
Life is like moonless nights;
And my poetry like withered lotuses
      on dead waters.
I am a rainless cloud of sorrow,
A dead thorn bush on the mountainside.

For years and years
My heart has been empty of desires.
Once I was a poet who praised beauty and love
      in his songs;
Alas, now I am absolutely silent,
More like a forgotten memory.

The day blossoms above the mountain,
And at dusk it withers
      in the silence of the plains;
So withered away the fleeting moments
      of my life
Like restless swallows in flight
Which fill the passers-by with grief
When they watch them disappear
      in the horizon.

Now with poetry, music and wine,
The goblet of my life, brimful of tears,
      I ask:
"Should one try to forget
      the torments of time
      by the help of wine?
"Should one give life a different colour
      by deception of poetry?
"Should one drown the cries of the spirit

in the sound of music?"
The space is full with my cries
But the sky, though it is all ears,
        is dead silent.
There is no companion around
        to whom I could say,
"Alas, wine no longer intoxicates me;
My goblet is left empty of pure poetry,
And my music is but cries in the wilderness.

In the far distance
The day gently blossoms
        above the mountain,
And rises, shining, high in the heavens;
Every particle of existence
        is a goblet brimmed
        with the wine of light,
But I am still left in the darkness
        of moonless nights;
A withered lotus on the lake of time,
And full of sorrow I ask:
"What if the goblet breaks?
What if the lute breaks?
What if poetry loses its charm?"

WHAT DUST?

The buds bear the promise of life,
Life itself is the opening of the buds.

Every Spring,
By the grace of bountiful clouds
All the boughs become full of buds,
And the buds unfold into blossoms,
And the blossoms,
        like multicoloured chandeliers,
Illuminate the trees,
And each tree appears like a whole garden.

When a newborn baby first opens its eyes,
It is a flourishing bud,
And, with cheeks sweeter than blossoms,
It illuminates the life of its parents;
Its face bears a Spring full of sweet songs
When it coyly smiles in its cradle.

Tell us, O travelling breeze,
By the ferocious *simoom* of what desert
These buds in the garden of life,
These blossoms of love,
Change, little by little, into thorns?
By the magic dust from what galaxy
These doves of peace and friendship
Transform into rabid wolves?

ON THE NIGHTS WHEN

On the nights when the sea
Pounded its head
Against the cliffs
Like disconsolate mourners;

On the nights when a bird
Full of sorrow,
Lonelier than the moon
Sang in a tree;

On the nights when the wind
Swinging its dagger
Shed the blood of poppies
On the meadow;

On the nights when the hearts
        of our friends burned
Like red sparks
Round the fire;

On the nights when we waited
In the desolate plain
To smell the scent
Of the fresh dawn;

On the nights when we walked,
Full of sorrow,
With our hearts burning
In the dreary rain;

Sadder than us
The eyes of stars
Had never seen
Anywhere on the Earth.

O the bright dawn,
My eyes and my heart
Are true mirrors
To your blessed face.

Come, come and see
How the horizons of the night
Are breaking up
By the burning cries of warriors.

IN THAT GOOD WORLD

Am I allowed to cast a glance
        from behind this wall,
At those colourful, bright blossoms?

Or, reaching through this fence
        of bloodstained barbed wire,
To take a drink of water
        from that burbling spring?

Or am I allowed to rest
        for a short while,

Here, by the door,
At the foot of the tree,
To regain a little strength?

Or must I be on the road,
        as I have always been,
        helpless and forlorn,
Bearing in my patient throat
        this centuries-old choking lump
        of *you-are-not-allowed*
        like a sharp dagger?

How wonderful it would be
If, in the expanses of shade and sun,
Under this blue dome,
Lands, waters and plants
Belonged to no one,
Or rather, they belonged
        to all people in the world:

The world of fellowmen,
        of friends;
The earth like a vast house,
        and the human beings
Like a single family,
        united
        by the warp and woof of life;
Together,
        and for each other,
With helpful hands,
        on the same footing.

In that beautiful world,
In all the green fields,
        with the horizons as their hedges;
In all the flower gardens,
        with gentle breezes as their walls;
Buds glowing with light and joy of love;
Songs making hearts throb with affection;
Smiles of gardeners shining like stars;
Jubilant cries of tillers rising to heavens:

In that wonderful world
We could all work
With our hearts full of desire for life;
With our faces blossoming like gardens of sweet briars;
With our eyes brimful of love.

We would sow love
Like seeds sown in the soil.
We would compose poems
As trees bear blossoms;
We would all be equals,
Singing and rejoicing,
Unchained, free and happy.

Siyâvash Kasrâ'i [Kowli]
(1926—1996)

ONE, TWO, THREE

One canary on the palm,
Two pigeons on the roof,
And three sparrows on the box tree;
There are no ties between them.
The explosion of an alarming sound
Is enough for the safety-loving birds
        to take a darting flight.

There explodes many a danger
        and the world is trembling
        with terror;
And you are alone in yourself,
We are all alone in ourselves.

DOMESTICATED

The bones thrown to us
From his festive table
Have made us loyal to him.

We fawn upon someone
Whose white trousers are well ironed
      everyday,
His shoes always shine,
And in his hand,
Adorned with several precious rings,
He always has a leather whip
      with a gold handle.

Sometimes we jump
And bark at him,
But we are careful not to raise
      his anger.

To tell the truth, we have become
      domesticated by him:
Spoiled, clownish and tame;
And among all who throng
      in his cookhouse,
There is not even one
      with a free spirit
      and a wild nature.

We have become domesticated dogs;
Ferocious wolves must come to the arena.

Mohammad Zohari
(1926—1995)

WITH A NEW SHADOW

The gullible man who wept
When he saw someone crying;
And smiled
When he saw someone smiling,
The old-timer, with his old shadow,
His old heart,
Is lying dead in the dust of his griefs,
His heart pierced with the dagger of despair.

Out of his putrid body
Another man has risen,
A man of stone, with the same old name
But with a new vision:
A man who only believes his own eyes;
Who laughs when others cry,
And weeps when others smile;
A new man with a new shadow,
          a new heart.

THE WELL OF THE WEST

They said,
"At the well of the East
There is no more an old water wheel
With something of a rope and bucket
So that every morning
It may raise the sun from the depth
     of darkness
To wash the crests of minarets
     with liquid gold."

They said,
"Now the East
Is mummified Pharaohs
In the dungeons of the Pyramids,
Or simple reliefs in some broken slabs
        and columns of stone
In the burnt-down Persepolis,
Or Prince Buddha
— The glorious image of silence —
In the wooded mountains of the Pamirs.

They said,
"The barren womb of the Old Mamma
        of the East
Can never be impregnated with any sperm
In expectation of another Moses,
        Jesus, or Mohammad."

They said,
"The East is dead and gone,
With no interrogations by the twin angels
Visiting the deceased
        at their first night in the grave, [10]
And with no resurrection on Judgement Day;
Now it is the West
That is the custodian of
        and the supervisor over
        the heritage of mankind
In every corner of the world,
With its ships of power in full sail
Enjoying favourable winds across
        the Seven Seas."

[10]   *The twin angels, called Monkar and Nakir, "are two fierce
looking angels who visit every man in his grave and who, immediately
after the return of the funeral party from the burial, are said to examine
the dead person as to his or her belief in God and Mohammad and to
torment him, if his answer is not satisfactory".* F.A. Klein, *The Religion
of Islam* (London, Curzon Press, 1979).

In search of treasures
We travelled on our feet of experience
Along the unmarked Silk Road [11]
To the perfumed bed chamber of the West,
— The stinky, painted strumpet —
But we found out
That there is also nothing new in the West.
It seems that everywhere the sky is blue;
The well of the West
Has no water wheel;
Now it is you and I,
        no one else,
And our blood is not redder
        or paler than that of the others;
We must travel over the mountain-path
Through the fortified wall
        of Gog and Magog; [12]
There is a way to the realm of peace;
The night has settled, starless and deep;
Take my hand, otherwise
We might lose each other on the way.

[11]   *The Silk Road, the ancient caravan route linking China with the West, passed through the neck of Kansu province in northern Iran.*

[12]   *Gog and Magog (Ya' juj and Ma' juj) are two giants, mentioned in the Koran. Among Iranian Moslems, there is a widely-known story that they lived in the land beyond China, where Alexander the Great built a fortified wall of iron or copper to protect the population from their marauding. The story goes that every day, when they wake up, Gog and Magog lick away at this wall until it is almost broken through but at sunset, exhausted, they fall asleep and the wall is restored to its original thickness by the next morning. However, at the end of time, before the advent of the Mahdi (the Absent or Twelfth Imam), when the anti-Mahdi (Dajjâl) appears, then Gog and Magog succeed in making a hole in the wall and pass through to join Dajjal in his mischief.*

LOST VOICE

I lost my voice,
My precious blossoming voice,
Which I had kept fresh with dewdrops
Gathered from pea leaves at dawn;
I lost my voice because
For too long I had kept hidden
      my song-flower,
— Which you said was wild but charming —
      in a dark corner
      of the house of silence.

Alas! I have even forgotten
The song my mother used to sing
Every time the canary of her heart
      fluttered for her mate;
The song I also sang
Whenever the canary of my heart
      fluttered with desire for my mate.
All the efforts of my larynx
      come to naught;
My vocal cords are poisoned;
I have lost my voice;
Who poured kohl in my wine? [13]

[13]   *Kohl, made from antimony or soot, is used to darken the edges of the eyelids. In the past, it was believed by some people that mixing kohl with someone's food or drink would make the victim lose his or her voice. It is said that some highly admired singers were given kohl by their rivals and lost their voices.*

Nosrat Rahmâni
(b. 1927)

OPIUM FLOWER

In the burning scent of sunshine
      in the plains of the East,
Where wheat, the golden grain of life,
The source of man's vital force, grows,
They say a poisonous flower blooms
Called Khashkhâsh.
He who smells it once
Becomes its slave for ever,
And is soon filled with aversion to existence.
It cures all maladies;
It cures death,
It cures life,
But is itself an incurable disease.

Wheat and white poppy
Sacrificed themselves
      to help man
      order his life;
One is a gift from God
And the other from Satan.

In the burning scent of sunshine
      in the plains of the East,
Where the flowers of feelings
      and poetry bloom,
Many poets sacrificed themselves
To wash away the sorrows of mankind.
They sacrificed themselves like wheat
To keep the wheels of life turning;
To free God's mind
From the rebellious ways of man.
Many ages passed
Until our day broke.

Now from this wanton dark world,
From this blind farmland,
There is no longer a path

to the spring of the sun;
And of those life-giving ears of wheat
Nothing is left
But some straws
in the hands of the wind;
Now not light, but plague
Pours from the sun;
And Satan himself sows Khashkhâsh
with the hands of God.

We are not to blame;
There is no longer a path
to the spring of the sun;
Any experienced tiller knows well
That there is no refuge for us
But sleep,
oblivion,
and silence.

BLASPHEMY

O God, have You ever kissed
The leaden lips of a drunk girl?
With Your teeth chattering
with temptation,
Have You ever touched her firm breasts?

O God, have You ever trembled
At the shrine of her bright eyes?
Or heard the cry of Your heart
In the darkness of her bosom?

O God, have You ever wept
When following black coffins?
Have Your silent eyes ever shed blood
rather than glances,
into someone else's eyes?

Alas! if You had feelings,
You would have lost Your heart,
And would also have made
A god for Yourself,
O godless God!

Bizhan Jalâli
(b. 1927)

IF ONLY A BIRD WOULD SING

If only a bird would sing
Or a flower would bloom
Into the darkness of my night;
If only a star would fall
Into the abyss of my despair;
If only the rebellion of my spirit
Could send all the people to sleep
And implore God to awake.

THE WORLD POURS INTO MY ROOM

The world pours into my room
       through the window
And through my eyes
       joins another world.
I am like a stream
Flowing between two fields.

MY ARMS ARE OPEN

My arms are open
To darknesses;
And the sun and the moon
Cannot quench the thirst
I bear in my bosom;
And I will only embrace Death
On the day when it will slide
Like a beloved
Into my arms.

OF THE DAY A BREATH IS LEFT

Of the day a breath is left
And of hope a day;
Of spirit a handful of dust is left
And of dust a smile;
Of all creation a shadow is left
And of shadows a sorrow;
Of the world a story is left
And of love a memory;
The rest is a regret as sweet
        as honey;
The rest is an unfinished regret.

A POET IS LIKE A DOVE

A poet is like a dove,
Flying over the darkness of the world
With its white wings,
Sometimes imagining
To have been carrying the stars
On its wings;
And sometimes thinking
That he takes the world with himself
To the heavens.

WITH THEIR FINGERS

With their fingers
The trees write on the sky
Something which they repeat
With their roots in the soil;
They speak of happiness.

O GOD OF DESTINY

O God of destiny,
How strangely you turn
The smile of a woman
Into a flower bud in my heart!
And how strangely
You make her glances
Flow in my heart
Like a river!
You have thrown me
Into such an ecstasy
That I dauntlessly walk
Through the heart of the world
And candidly speak!

I HEAR THE VOICE OF DEATH

I hear the voice of death
Which is pleasant and overpowering,
And say to myself,
— It is a friend calling me! —
And go on my way;
But still its voice
Echoes in my ears.

EVERY GREEN LEAF

Every green leaf
Is a window, open
From man's heart to the world,
And a message of friendship
Between the earth and the sun;
Every green leaf
Is a promise
Of immortality
When we are thinking
Of our dark end.

Simin Behbahâni
(b. 1928)

YOU SAID IT WAS GRAPES

"It is grape," you said.
      "No, it isn't!" I said.

"Believe me," you said,
      "I'm going to pick a bunch.
This is the vineyard of history,
      and these vines yield
Plenty of grapes every year ..."

Your hands were moving,
      as if you were picking.
"I've no liking for jokes!" I said.
"Close your eyes," you said,
      "And open your mouth.
Now you are going to taste
      this delicate, sweet fruit."

I did what you asked,
      and then I exclaimed:
      "Ugh ! how sour it is!"
I felt sick with its taste of blood.
I threw it out;
      it was an eye
      pulled out of its socket.
It was as if I were caught
      by a landslide;
In my eyes horizons began to turn
      like a millstone;
Rain of blood fell from the moon
      and the Pleiades ... [14]

[14]   *In classical Persian poetry, the seven stars of the Pleiades are likened to a bunch of grapes or a necklace. Simin Behbahâni uses this old image because she is writing in the form of a "ghazal".*

You said, "It's grapes"
    but I persisted in my cries,
"I cannot see on the vines
        anything but eyes
        pulled out of their sockets!"

OH! I MADE LOVE!

Oh! I made love
        with a hideous beast
In a nightmare,
        lost in delirium.

Both awake and asleep,
        with desire and disgust;
Hands,
        while fighting,
        passionately embracing;
Lips,
        while kissing,
        furiously cursing;
Full of hate and love,
        so sickened, so overjoyed,
With a gazelle, so graceful,
        but fallen dead in a desert.

Oh, even the thought of it
        makes me nauseous;
Was I so drunk
        that I could quench my thirst
With fetid water
        in a crystal cup!
Only a strong fire
        can cleanse my being
Of this damnable filth;
I must throw myself
        into a furnace.

I wish I could become a snake
        and could cast off my skin,

Escaping from myself
    with a shining, new body.

But, alas! I am unsaveable
        like a naked sword,
Rusted to the core
    in the slime of hell.
I run away, but my body
    runs along with me,
For my body is myself,
    and I,
    a tired fugitive,
    belong to it.

Oh! the love I made
    was like tossing a coin
    with two heads,
One bearing the figure of Gabriel,
    the other of Satan!

PERHAPS IT IS THE MESSIAH

The horizon's womb is rich
    with the embryo of light;
The blind darkness will certainly give birth
    to its beloved child, the Sun.

Tomorrow the blue dome
    will be shining
By the light of the bright morning,
    the very morning now
    far beyond the vision of your belief.

Tomorrow the glorious face of the Sun
    above the snow-clad mountain
Will bring to your mind
    the image of a fresh dahlia
    in a crystal vase.

What you see now
        across the wet, clean firmament
Is not only a rainbow,
        but also the triumphal arch of light.

A shaft of sunbeams
        has pierced the clouds;
Perhaps it is the Messiah
        strolling through the heavens.

Is it hope? Is it joy? Whatever it is,
        it cannot be air;
I am breathing pure happiness,
        pure delight.

The loving meadows of our friends' eyes
        radiate mirth,
Like an open-air festival of flowers,
        with colours shining in the sun.

In the garden of my heart
        the rose bush of belief has bloomed;
Morning is here, I swear by God!
        it is no deception, no vanity.

GRACEFULLY SHE APPROACHED

Gracefully she approached,
        in a dress of bright blue silk;
With an olive branch in her hand,
        and many tales of sorrows in her eyes.
Running to her, I greeted her,
        and took her hand in mine:
Pulses could still be felt in her veins;
        warm was still her body with life.

"But you are dead, mother", I said;
        "Oh, many years ago you died!"
Neither of embalmment she smelled,
        Nor in a shroud was she wrapped.

I gave a glance at the olive branch;
        she held it out to me,
And said with a smile,
        "It is the sign of peace; take it."

I took it from her and said,
        "Yes, it is the sign of ...", when
My voice and peace were broken
        by the violent arrival of a horseman.
He carried a dagger under his tunic
        with which he shaped the olive branch
Into a rod and looking at it
        he said to himself:
"Not too bad a cane
        for punishing the sinners!"
A real image of a hellish pain!
        Then, to hide the rod,
He opened his saddlebag.
        In there, O God!
I saw a dead dove, with a string tied
        round its broken neck.

My mother walked away with anger and sorrow;
        my eyes followed her;
Like the mourners she wore
        a dress of black silk.

THE FRAGRANCE OF MY EYES

Without you I am nothing,
        nothing,
Like a year deprived of its days;
Without you I am empty,
        empty,
Like an almond shell without its kernel.
O you who guard my innocence,
As fragrance is kept in the firm fist of a bud;
You who have given me shelter
In the heart of your peaceful seclusion;

You who are the truest of all measures
        for comparison;
Seeing you, I have seen
Thousands of galaxies of suns
In the sphere of my night.
O you in me the power of my intoxication,
The fire of all my passion,
I have filled my cup for you
With the blood of grapes
        from the vineyard of life.

The fragrance of my eyes, my narcissi, [15]
With the breeze of my glances
Take messages
To the green Spring of your eyes.
I will sleep in you
Like a drop of rain in a deep sea;
In you I will search
Both for my beginning and my end.

I have reached the autumn of my life,
Yet I have created Spring in my heart;
How astonished I am
By my untimely blossoming.
In my body flow
Hundreds of springs of red and green light;
With you I have a colourful ecstasy of illusions.

No other hands except yours
Have ever become intimate
With my body;
Though I am lawfully known
By some other man's surname.

[15]   *The use of the narcissus as a metaphor for a woman's eye —
particularly of someone who is drunk, sleepy or suffering an illness —
is as old as Persian poetry itself. Hâfez of Shirâz, the great 13th century
master of the lyrical ghazal form, wrote: "by the charm of your
intoxicating narcissus and of your wine-worshipping ruby/You threw
Hâfez, who was a recluse, into the impiety of wine".*

Hassan Honarmandi
(b. 1928)

THE DAUGHTER OF THE SEA

At the time
> when kisses flutter
> upon the lips of the breeze,
She is taken out of her mother's arms,
Bathed with the fragrances of the morning;
And her hammock is hung on the waves;
The wind sings in her ears,
And the sea strews her feet
> with thousands of pearls.

Many a spring will pass like this,
And then,
> one morning,
> in the early spring,
When kisses flutter
> upon the lips of the breeze
On a road sprinkled with my tears,
It will be said that a girl
> has lost her heart to me;
That I have lost my heart to a girl.

Many a spring will pass like this.

One night the breeze will lament
> in the far distance;
And they will say
> that a woman's bed chamber
Turned into a grave for her.

COLOURS

I said that Red
      is the colour of our time,
Though Green is the colour
      which fascinates me;
Yet a new song is heard, saying:
"There is no colour beyond Black." [16]

EPITAPH

One day all of you will gather
      round this grave,
And will whisper of something new.
In that day, sing this line
      in my memory:
"I hate everybody, and I hate myself
      more than all!"

You will shed a few drops
      of futile tears on my dust,
And among you not even one
      would tread the path of piety.
Suddenly a murmur will rise
      from inside the grave, saying:
"I hate everybody and I hate
      this remembrance of yours as well!"

[16] *A Persian proverb, meaning the situation is hopeless and cannot get any blacker.*

Houshang Ebtehâj [H.E. Sâyeh]
(b. 1928)

THE SIGH OF THE MIRROR

They recognized her by her long hair.

O Earth, is this the same pure body?
Is man nothing but a handful of dust?

When she combed her long hair,
She let her imagination fly
In the boundless sphere of the mirror.

Smiling, with the morning *salaam*, [17]
She lifted her hand to her hair,
Drew the night aside,
And watched the sun in the mirror.

The thought of the rising day
Poured a shower of stars
Into the sky of her young eyes.
Then her sweet smile
Opened to the mirror
The gate of the sunny garden
      of her spirit.

Oh, the scorched spring,
The ashes of youth,
The flown-away image of the empty mirror;
With the memory of your long hair
The mirror sighs in the dust of dawn.

The birds in the garden sang,
      but in vain;
It was not the season of roses.

[17]   *The Arabic word of greeting, meaning "peace"*.

THE END FOR A NEW BEGINNING

I closed the gates of my poems on you
  O Gâlie [18], sovereign of the ancient land of my poetry!

I took down the dead candelabrum
Which once gave light to the memory of your eyes
In the dusty sanctum of my poetry,
To light a sun brighter than the diamond of your eyes;

To give rise to a day
Warmer than the throbs of your heart;
To awake a breeze
More refreshing than the sweet smell of your breaths.

And I no longer want to hear
Your nocturnal songs
At the gate of this lofty palace,
O Galie, the damned love!

I do not want to open
The gate of my poetry
To anyone but a comrade,
O, Galie, queen of my dreams.

And now I cry:
"Come, you naked bodies,
Clad in shirts of blue kisses of whips;
Come, you the arms of labour,
Stroked by the blood-stained links of chains;
Here is the city of my poetry
Which I grant to you.

"Compose my poems
With the warm blood of life:
Glorious as labour,
And sweet as hope.

[18] *Gâlie or Gâliyâ is the name of a woman, and used by H. Ebtehâj*
(H.E. Sâyeh) in at least two of his poems as a symbolic beloved of the poet.

"We will divert the stream of dawn
That has been flowing
Far away from the desert of our night.

"And with canals of blood
We will join our dark homeland
To the bright oceans."

And you, the woman whom I do not know,
Lull your glances to sleep
In the eyes of love
By the lullabies of restraint;
And wake your blood
In the veins of labour,
Until I find the word
That tastes of fire!

PICTURE

The empty house of loneliness
Resembling a mirror
        with no reflections
Throughout the sombre night
        of endurance.

A picture hung on the wall
Like a green memory
In the mind of an autumn night.

A girl
With her head held high,
        with a cascade of soft hair;
A boy
The silent sorrow of his father
        in his eyes;
And a woman, elegant but detached ...

In the sombre night of endurance
        a lonely man
Like a mirror with no reflections,
The emptiness of the house of loneliness.

A silent shadow cries
In the dark night of the mirror.
Ah, a hundred pictures
Will never fill
The empty place
        of those gentle footsteps
        on the carpet.

It is the mirror
        that is crying with you;
And you are nothing
        but the lonely image.

Sohrâb Sepehri
(1928—1980)

THE MOTION OF THE WORD LIFE

Beyond the pinewood, snow;
Snow, and a flock of crows.
The road means emigration;
Wind, sounds, traveller,
             and feeling like having some sleep.
Ivy foliage, arrival, and
        stepping into the backyard.

I and my gloomy heart,
        and these wet windowpanes.
I am writing, and two walls,
        and several sparrows.

Someone is sad;
Someone is weaving;
Someone is counting;
Someone is singing.

Life means a starling took wing.
What has made you unhappy?
Pleasant things are not scarce;
        for instance, the sun
        that shines there;
The child of the day-after-tomorrow;
Or the pigeons of last week.

Drops of water falling;
Snow lying on the shoulder of silence;
And time on the spine
        of the white jasmine.

ADDRESS

It was dawn when the man on the horse
    asked,
"Where is the friend's house?"

The passer-by gave the branch of light
    he had between his lips
    to the darkness of the sands;
And pointing to a poplar tree, he said:

"Before reaching that tree,
There's an orchard path
    greener than God's dreams
Where love is as blue
    as the feathers of Sincerity;
Beyond the end of the path
    stands Maturity;
There you turn towards
    the Solitude flower;
Two steps before the flower
You will stop at the eternal myths
    of the earth
And there you will be filled
    with a transparent fear.
You will hear a rustle
    in the flowing sincerity
    of the space:
You will see a small boy
    who has climbed
    a tall pine tree
    to pick a fledgling
    from the nest of light;
You will ask him
    where the house of the friend is."

FRIEND

She was great: [19]
She was of the inhabitants of Today,
And had relationship
     with all the vast horizons;
And how well she could understand
     the dialects of Water and Soil!

Her voice
Was like the confused melancholy of Reality;
And her eyelids
Showed us the way
     to the pulsation of the Elements;
And her hands
Leafed through the clear sky of Generosity;
And she persuaded Love
     to move to our neighbourhood.
She was like her seclusion,
And interpreted to Mirrors
The most amorous curves of her Time;
And like rain, in her attitude,
     she was brimming with the freshness
     of Repetition;
And, like trees, in her behaviour,
She spread in the serenity of Light.
She always called the childhood of the Wind,
And tied the string of talk
To the latches of Water.

One night
She expressed to us
The green prostration of Affection
     in such a clear way
That we could touch

[19]   *It is said that Sohrâb Sepehri wrote this poem in memory of Forugh Farrokhzâd, the poetess who died in a car accident in 1967. In Sepehri's book, the poem has the epigraph from T.S. Eliot: "I should be glad of another death".*

the sentiments on the surface
of the Earth;
And felt refreshed
like the accent
of a pail of water.

And many a time we saw her
carrying many baskets,
When she was on her way
to pick the grapes of Good Tidings.

But she did not happen to sit
Before the clarity of Doves
And went to the edge of Nothingness
And lay down
behind the patience of Lights;
And had no idea
That for having eaten an Apple [20]
How miserably we were left alone
In the clamour created
by the utterance of Doors!

[20]　*A reference to mankind's first sin in the Garden of Eden, though for Moslem Iranians the forbidden fruit is believed to be wheat rather than an apple.*

Mehdi Akhavân Sâless [M. Omid]
(1928—1990)

GREEN

Where did I go with you last night?
Up to the presence of God,
    and beyond His wilderness
    I journeyed with you.
I would not say that angels flew
    wing to wing with me;
Nor would I say that rain of gold
    fell on me;
But, O green scent, fostered in the shade,
O fairy whom the wind took away
From the flower-studded silken meadows
    of the curtain,
With you I went to the realm
    of the green shades,
To the springtime of the meadows of fragrance,
To a land whose strangeness
    was familiar to my eyes.

Along with you I went to Solitude,
    to Freedom,
Along with you who took me away,
— Away from the presence
and the absence of Self —.

Riding with you who raced with light
In your glorious *howdah* [21] of mysteries and songs,
    of comprehension and astonishment,
Towards the furthest frontiers
    of the remotest regions,
— You, the green barley of my impatient steed,

[21]   *A seat or covered pavilion on the back of an elephant or camel, used in the past for travelling, especially for women.*

The open fan of my passionate peacock,
My dearest bondage,
        my emerald chain of pleasant poison.

The chambers of my memory full of strokes
        and twinkles of light,
Violent waves the safest bridges under
        my feet;
There were mysteries and meditations.
With all the burden of Existence,
With all the comfort of Forgiveness,
My journey took me to the realm
        of His justice
In whose scales esteem, rejection
        and mourning are the same.

All the *whats* and *whys* died in my heart
Because to the Unquestionable I went.
I give you my tearful thanks,
Blessed be your home,
        my dear green waste,
You whose ring with emerald signet
        is a plaything of the winds,
Where did you take me last night?
How far away did I go with you last night?

CONVERSATION

" ... Well, that's how the story goes.
And I have even heard tell
Of heavy rain,
Followed by a powerful flood,
Which washed away the borderlines,
And did away with barriers.
I have also been told
That there, freedom of flight
Filled the space;
Bridges are no longer founded
        on illusions;

Now narrow is the gap between hands
        and desires;
It is even no longer impossible
        to be decent
        and yet to survive.
The dreams of fairy tales
        have come true;
Blue birds of happiness which only flew
        in fairy lands
Have now perched there,
        on the roofs, calling:
'O you, whoever you are,
Come, come and fill up your baskets
        with whatever you wish!'
And I have also heard tell of ...
What! why are you laughing?
I am a simple peasant,
I breathe with truth;
I can't believe
        that you don't believe me!"

"Well, you are absolutely right;
Such a happy land is really a wonder!
But
I have dreamed,
Thou hast dreamed,
He has dreamed,
We have ..."

"Enough!"

UP THERE

At the lunch table
I was poisoning myself as usual
With one or two goblets
Of my stinging, deadly booze,
Taking as nibbles
The bitter, burning lip-biting

Of one who,
        with all the world,
Still feels alone.

The little boy,
        — my son —
Had gone up there,
In the nook above two rows of bookshelves,
With his hands stretched on both sides,
Leaning on his elbows,
His palms open,
His legs hanging down,
And his head lifted up,
Like a cross made of rough wood,
Or, if I must avoid a rough similization,
Perhaps like a crucified man.

"Come down, Zardosht," said his sister, [22]
"It's time to go to bed;
"Come down, I'm sleepy!"
"I won't come down,"
        said the Zardosht of the cross;
I told him, or I should have told him,
"You come down, son!
"Your father must sleep up there!"
Or perhaps,
"Up there your father is asleep!"

[22]   *In the poem, Zardosht is the name of the poet's son but, as he is drunk and lonely, the poet sees the image of Zardosht (Zoroaster or Zarathustra), founder of the Zoroastrian religion, mixed with the image of Jesus Christ on the cross. Though he never denied being a Moslem, Akhavân Saless was deeply interested in ancient Persian civilisation and its religions.*

Nâder Nâderpur
(b. 1929)

THE FALSE DAWN

Tonight the earth has said goodbye
To all its sins;
The white piety of snow
Has concealed the infidelities of men.
This silvery mask
On the dark face of Nature
Is the most beautiful of lies in the world.

Tonight the old tree
Thinks it is still young,
But after the birth of the sun
Its snow-like thoughts will melt away.

Where is the eye that can see
The face of the concealed truth?
Perhaps only eyes well washed with tears
Can have such a claim.

O old tree!
What a torrent of tears is the rain!
A weeping as vast as the sorrow of the sky
Over the negligence of the earth;
Tears that darken the false dawn of the snow
At the dusk of your transient youth,
But they take you back
Nearer to the light of childhood;
Tears that can give the eyes of an old man
A sight as clear as that of
        the childlike eye of the sun.

O, the rooster anxiously waiting
        for the day to break,
Fire will never die in a bed of cotton;

But look!
The sun has died in the whiteness
          of the horizons.
The spell of the snow
Has filled the eyes of the simple trees
          with sleep;
Has led the meek peasants in their old age
To the city of imaginary youth
On a steed of illusions.
But the heart of the earth
Is full of desire for the weeping of the sky;
There is a truth concealed in the night.

O, the sorrow darker than clouds!
Help me with a ceaseless weeping tonight;
O affectionate tears!
Give my eyes the clear sight of a child.

FROM BEHIND THE FLAMES

She was with me in my house,
And the crimson fire
Was blazing in the fireplace;
From behind the reflection of the flames
          the outline of her shape
Dancing like smoke,
Twisting like a snake,
Telling the tale of my life
          with her every movement:

That night, in that remote tavern,
Where the drunken had fallen asleep,
Where the moonlight,
          like pure wine,
Filled the goblets,
She was with me,
          and I was intoxicated
          by her wine;
Her figure, like a dark blue flame,

Gleamed in the black smoke of her shadow;
In my smile throbbed her kisses;
In her kisses faded away her smile;
And in the serene seclusion of the night
She yielded her body to desire;
With my lips I picked jasmines and roses
        from her breasts,
And she lay in my arms,
        more naked than the moon,
And I, like a snake,
        slithered down to her treasure.

Alone I am in my room tonight,
But her image is here with me,
And the fire with crimson flames
Burning as before in the fireplace;
And her tall figure,
        in the reflection of the flames
Dancing like smoke,
Twisting like a snake,
Is telling me the tale of my life
        with remembrance of the past.

NIGHT AND THE WHISPERS OF THE BOATS

How clear is the sea!
How calm is the sea tonight!
The moonlight has spread
The shadows of the palm trees on the shore
Like carpets of pure silk.

What gives ripples to the deep silence
Is only the splashing of the boats,
As they whisper into each other's ears
About the amorous hugs and kisses
        of the sea and the shore.

The great spirit of water,
        in her sweet dreams,

Opens her arms to a bright morning;
But, as for me,
    there comes the vision
    of my childhood land
And banishes sleep from my tired eyes;
And then, at the threshold of my old age,
A door opens to the tormenting days of affliction.

In the far distance,
    I see the soil of my homeland
    drenched in blood,
And there, in the sky,
    I watch the sun in the agony of death;
There, when the Spring migrates
    and the Moon goes into exile,
Nothing remains but the Winter
    and its boundless night.

There, in my homeland,
    while there is no mention
    of the Spring of Life [23]
In the reigning darkness
    deadly stories of bestial madness
    do happen everywhere.
The light in the eyes of people
Is wilder than the glitter
    in the eyes of the beasts.

In my homeland,
    the regicidal millers of history
Have a stigma of catastrophic treason
    on the forehead;

[23]   *In Persian folklore and legend, the Water of Life is a spring flowing through the Land of Darkness and a drink from it gives man eternal life. Alexander the Great is said to have found the spring but his two attempts to drink the water from it ended in failure. Only the prophet Elijah (known as Khezr) succeeded in drinking from the spring and he is said to be still alive. Nâder Nâderpur refers to the situation in Iran when he speaks of darkness and there being no Spring of Life.*

And the Caliph Omar is always victorious
       over Yazdegerd the Ill-fated; [24]
And the dawn of Tomorrow
Is as dark and melancholy
       as the end of Today.

In my homeland,
       the merciless, insatiable desert,
Is so intoxicated with blood
       that it will not sober up for thousands of years;
And whoever speaks of the Sun
       is a fireworshipper [25]
In the eyes of those Bedouinophils.

In my homeland,
       the true pious folk are trees;
With their praying hands
       raised towards the dark heavens,
Their trembling fingers
       search for God in despair.

In my homeland
For the women,
       veiled as desert-dwellers,
       and confined to the tents,
Enjoying sunshine in the open is only a dream.
Though bearing children has always been
       a sacred passion in their nature,
Fearing lest their sons join the martyrs

[24]   *Yazdegerd, the last of the Sassanid kings, did his best to stop the Arabs invading Persia but, after several defeats, he fled to Marv, a town in the north-east of the Persian Empire. But the governor of Marv decided to betray him and the king was killed by one of his own people in a miller's hut. He is always known as Yazdegerd the Ill-fated. The invasion of Iran took place in the reign of Omar ibn al Khattab (581-644), the second Moslem caliph in succession to Abu Bakr.*

[25]   *Zoroastrians never worshipped fire, which for them was a purifying element of Nature, giving light in darkness and warmth in the cold. Nâder Nâderpur is here referring to the naive Moslems who are fundamentally ignorant of other religions.*

in their thousands,
They no longer cherish
the desire of motherhood.

In my homeland
the balance of justice
is in the hand of Death,
And the close friend of the *grave* is the *cradle*;
So, only by dying can a man attain
some value for his life;
And those still alive
have no security and peace of mind
in their mournful abode.
In my homeland
there is a secret passage
from your house to the prison,
The passage between your heart and your tongue;
If you have a secret, it is unwise
to reveal it where
your beloved son is present.

In my homeland
love and wine are fallen from grace;
If love comes to you,
you should not open your heart to her;
And of wine if only a cupful
is left in your flagon,
Let it be shed like tears in the dust.

In my homeland
as the custom commands among the Arabs, [26]
Devilishly cruel is the lash
to the naked back of the drunk;

[26]   *Nâder Nâderpur clearly means Moslems when he writes of "the Arabs". In the following stanzas, he protests at the Islamic punishment for drunkenness and robbery, while social justice is ignored. The Mufti (mentioned later) is a theologian learned in Islamic law, known among the Shi' ah as an Ayatollah, and the poet has in mind the excesses that happened after the Islamic Revolution. But this should not be used to make a judgement on Islam as a whole, for over the centuries theologians have delivered conflicting opinions on many issues, including the question of whether music and poetry are contrary to Islamic law.*

And judges can condemn the guilty
      to be thrown from the mountain tops
Down on the jagged rocks.

In my homeland
      you must not follow Eve and Adam
      in their lust for life,
For they are thought to have deserved
      to be cleansed of their sins
      with their own blood.
There, though it is the wealthy
      who rob the poor
      of the fruits of their toil,
The fingers of the robbed are cut by Justice.

In my homeland
According to the Mufti's gospel
      the Pen is a bondslave;
The touch of flutes on the musicians' lips
      is deemed to be venom to life;
The poets' Muses are cursed as demons;
And the artists' creative purpose
      is known to be idolatry.

There, in my homeland,
      you do not expect to see
      even the Moon naked,
      bathing in a pond.
Yes, in the far distance,
      I see the soil of my homeland
      drenched in blood;
And there, in the sky,
      I watch the sun in agony of death.

How clear is the sea!
How calm is the sea tonight!
The moonlight has spread
The shadows of the palm trees on the shore
Like carpets of pure silk.

The drunk man walking
        on this slippery road,
— Falling and rising, in the dusky night —
Who in the mirrors of the foreign guesthouses
Is seen with my face,
        and bearing my name,
Is a wretched soul
        far away from his homeland;
Who, at night, lays his head on my pillow,
Not aware at all
        of the tormenting fire in him
By the smoke of which,
        time and time again,
        my eyes have been in tears;
And through its flames
        it has covered my head with ashes.

A WINGED HEART

The shadow of a winged heart
Enshrouded the earth
On a moonlit night of Spring.

Darkness fell on the tresses of trees,
On the eyes of the windows,
On the breasts of the walls.

The somnolent force
Exuding from the vast shadow
Fell on the lifeless
And the living.

"This must be an eclipse," they said,
"Yes, a total eclipse!
We must beat copper;
Hasten to the roof with a copper washtub!" [27]

[27]   *This is a reference to the superstitious belief that an eclipse of the moon is caused by Satan covering the moon with his hand and beating something like a copper washtub may frighten Satan away.*

The terror of the winged heart
On the moonlit night of Spring
Had seized the whole world.

No one turned his head
To cast a glance at the moon
Except for one small boy,
                              who
— Startled from sweet sleep —
Said that he could see
A bluebottle
        sitting on the moon. (28)

MORNING SONG

In the shy blue sky
A bird cried:
"Where is it, then?
Where is the Morning?"
"It is on your wings,"
I said in reply.

And the bird flew away;
        and the Morning bloomed
        in my eyes.

(28)   *A bluebottle sitting on the moon is a reference to the poet Ahmad-Rezâ Ahmadi, who as a teenager began publishing poems with unusual and surrealist imagery and an emphatic disregard for anything conventional in Persian poetry. Nâderpur implies that it was this "small boy" who, when many poets were groping about to find their way in the eclipse between the traditional and the modern, pointed to the moon and said that he could see a bluebottle sitting on it.*

Manuchehr Âtashi
(b. 1931)

ONE TO FIVE

I

On the dome,
        pigeons were a flock of dewdrops;
Behind the hill,
        red poppies were fire;
When my glance became an angel,
When my glance trembled,
Rain began to fall.

II

O the sky of my childhood
Will you give my mischievous eyes
        rainbows again?
Will you place the sparrows
Within range of my catapult again?
Will you give the appetite
        of my wooden horse
        the fragrant spring again?

III

The well is uselessly waiting;
The black wind of gunpowder
Has taken wings
        towards the mountain;
Newspapers write about the plague ...
In the mountain a snowstorm ...

IV

The night pulsates
Like a sick man's heart,
With the beat

of my dark-blooded dreams;
And the pencil between
        my burnt fingers ...
And poetry
On the other side of the street
Aimlessly walks under young trees.

V

O my untidy bed,
Of the virgins
Which one is our guest tonight?

Too long has the world been waiting
        for a new prophet.

PERHAPS

Ghosts
Alighted from the winds
As they were passing by the huts
Scattered along the coast.

Perhaps the wild winds have a story
Which can bestow many blessings
On those poor huts.

Perhaps the winds
Have a tragic story
Which can draw the fish dead
        to the surface.

Perhaps from the winds
A great man,
A saviour will rise ...

Perhaps
There is a story with the winds;
Perhaps the winds ...
Are only winds after all ...

Yadollâh Royâ'i
(b. 1932)

SEAMARKS [III]

Silence was a bunch of flowers
Inside my throat;
The song of the seashore
Was the breeze of my kisses
     and your open eyelids.
Over the waters the bird of the wind
Was confused in the nest
    of a thousand voices.
Over the waters
The bird was restless.

The sound of the wet thunder and light,
The wet light of the lightning,
Turned the water into a mirror
Framed in the flames of the sea.

The breeze of kisses,
    your eyelids,
     and the bird of the wind
Turned into fire and smoke
    in my throat,
And the silence was a bunch of flower.

SEAMARKS [XXX]

O Sea!
The turbulent innocence
    in the waters of disaster,
    waters of terror;
The waters of a thousand plaits,
    a thousand eyelids,

The waters of a thousand adventures
      in the faraway straits;
The waters of the rooms with closed doors
      in the solitude of the petrified birds.
The labyrinthine corridors
Which concealed felonies and misdemeanours
      in their recesses.

The waters of liberty without law,
In the land of repetitions
Full of rights and volition.

from LABIAL VERSES

78

My passage fills with life
      when you sit;
I become the life of passage;
A target for your life
      in your sitting.

At the time of your sitting
I become the passage of time;
I become time
So that you pass me
      wherever you sit.

118

[My mother's passing]

She had a thousand leaves of breast;
She gave her thousand leaves of breast
To the shadow,
And the shadow,
      that was dragging her away,
Had a thousand mirrors in its hands;
A thousand leaves of breast
Became a finite body;
Became the infinite bodies.

Farrokh Tamimi
(b. 1933)

DOORS AND WALLS

We are two walls,
Two high walls in a narrow street.
The hands of a builder,
Who was perhaps called Destiny,
— Or call it whatever you like —
Laid the bricks of our youth
And laughed;
Our hearts began to moan
In the clay of each brick.

We are two walls;
For many years,
        day and night,
We have been watching the hastening passers-by,
Some whispering into each other's ears,
Some bearing their loneliness.

We are two walls and in us
The eyelids of all the doors are
        eternally closed.
Whenever rises the breeze of some talking
Somewhere in the street,
The eyelids of the doors gently move
With the illusory feeling
Of an unseen stroking hand;
But, alas, the hand
Keeps the eyelids of the doors closed
With the dream of an opening.

Moments and eyelids heavy as lead.

We are two walls,
Two high walls in a narrow street,

Standing close to each other,
But in separation we shall die;
We are under the power
Of the Master builder, Destiny!

GENESIS

The black dust of the night
Fell from the heavens,
Sad as the withered smile
On the lips of the Messiah;
From the evergreen garden of Eden,
Spread out eastwards,
Two lines of light shone
      like two crystalline arms:
Two lines of light that seemed
To be waiting for the advent of a body.

The blessed breeze blew
      from the north of the garden;
A woman blossomed;
Her arms two lines of light,
And in the Eastern garden of Thought
The Book of Genesis took form
With shining words.

"And the spirit of God
Moved upon the face of waters." [29]

---

[29] *The quotation is from the Book of Genesis. Using quotations from the Koran, especially in didactic and mystical poetry, is not new but quoting from the Bible and the scriptures of other religions is one of the new tendencies in modern Persian poetry.*

Bahman Forsi
(b. 1933)

HELLO!

Now a word with the wall,
A word with the earth:
"Is anybody there?"

Here no one says Hello to anybody.
In the canon of this civilization
The current lesson
Is the absurdity of Hello;
And the valid coin,
Minted in the Fast Food Factory,
Is Alienation.

You cannot pay
The cash of Morality
Into any bank account;
No pawnbroker gives a penny
For your robe of Dignity;
And your Honesty of a lifetime
Fails to convince any grocer
For a few pounds of potatoes.

Ohhhhh!
Who was it?
        When was it?
                Where was it?
Where was the land whose inhabitants
Believed in the observance of saying Hello?
With Hello they opened their eyes;
With Hello every house joined the alleys;
With Hello every alley joined the streets.

When going on a visit,
Just on arrival,
Once the feet touched the threshold,

Everyone,
      child or adult,
Was in a hurry to be first
      to say Hello.
Schoolgirls, at least,
      would utter: "Hellll ..."
And the punks of the neighbourhood,
Would rumble: "Lllllo!"

Ohhhhh!
Who was it?
      When was it?
            Where was it?
How soon it all passed!
How soon it all ended!

ILLUSIONIA

Everything that I wanted,
But I was always denied to have them:

A drop of freedom,
Of hope,
Of future;
A breath of happiness,
Of confidence,
Of certainty;

All these things
In the warnings of Politics,
In the suggestions of Religion,
Were promised to be granted
      in Illusionia,
Somewhere far beyond Esidarap. [30]

[30] *The name the poet has given to the land of promises is "Nowhere-on-earth-only-in-mind" which some religions interpret as Paradise. In view of the satirical tone of the poem, the translator suggested writing "Paradise" backwards — as Samuel Butler did for Nowhere in his Utopian novel "Erewhon" — and the poet found this appropriate.*

There you will have everything,
But you will laugh
At the idea of having them;
There you will be offered everything,
But you will not take anything;
There is no Forbiddance,
No Chastisement;
And Law does not mean Compulsion.

But no one knew
Where Illusionia was;
It was neither
     on the other side
of the Mount Qâf,[31]
Nor at the end
     of the Sindbad's Eighth Voyage.[32]
But everybody believed
That, at this very moment,
On this very earth,
It really existed.

My mother had heard her mother,
Quoting her grandmother,
Calling it Nowhere-In-The-World;
And one of her ancestresses
Had mentioned it as Illusionia.

Ever since man began
To have soul in his body,

[31]   *Mount Qâf (Ghâf) is a legendary mountain, said to be the highest in the world and made of green crysolite. Some scholars believe that Qâf is the Caucasus Mountains which were thought to surround the earth, so that no one had ever seen beyond them.*

[32]   *Sindbad the Sailor (or Sindbad of the Sea), in one of the tales of the Thousand and One Nights, is a rich young man of Baghdad who makes seven sea voyages as a merchant and experiences many adventures. His eighth voyage cannot be anywhere but in the other world. In fact, in this poem Bahman Forsi mentions the "Haft-Khân", or Seven Adventures from Ferdowsi's Book of Kings, an image which is far less known to Western readers than the story of Sindbad.*

And illusion in his mind,
Illusionia existed.

But my father,
A sceptic, a materialist,
Who had used up the Earth's patience,
Who did not care a damn about Heaven,
Did the best he could,
Strained his every nerve,
To make me understand
That no such damned place existed at all.

But I always closed the eyes of my reason
And took refuge
In the darkest depths of illusion
Lest the undeveloped film of my Illusionia
Be exposed to Light;
Lest my flickering hope die away.

HUMAN

In my fleeting life
What I could learn is that
One either is Human,
Or isn't;
And the idea
          of confining men's identity
To geographical names
Is not compatible
With soundness of mind.

Iranians are kind to their servants!
The Swiss are very mean!
The English are tricksters!
Russians are hardheaded!
All these judgements,
If not nonsense,
Are really a load of rubbish!

If you think carefully,
You will see that,
          say, Alaska

Has also its tricksters,
Or Sweden also its windbags,
Or Tibet its scoundrels,
Or Morocco its hoodlums;
Having this or that character
Hasn't much to do
With one's homeland.

What I think is that
Man paves the way for man;
Man shouldn't be afraid of man;
Man is destined to love man;
Yet I don't really understand
Why man kills man!
Why man buys man!
Why man sells man!
But I very well know
That all these
Are neither the effects
Of Geography,
Nor the work
Of God Almighty!

DRINK

Not green,
Nor blue,
Poetry must be like a virgin.
After a drink
Become bare of yourself
And sleep with her;
Reading and listening to poetry
Spoils it.

REUNION

The earth has one body
And tomorrow
My body will be earth again
And no matter where they inter you,
You will rest in my arms.

Mahmud Mosharraf Âzâd Tehrâni [M. Âzâd]
(b. 1933)

UNTITLED

It is not only man who loves;
The sea and sails,
      the sun and fields,
      are all blessed with love.
It is not only man ...

It is not only man who cries;
I have seen birds,
I have seen leaves,
      and winds,
      and rain
         crying.
It is not only man ...

It is not only man who sings;
I have heard songs
      from stones,
      from plants;
I have heard with my own ears
      the winds and leaves
      singing.

But it is only man
      who has loneliness
      without end;
It is only man
      whose deadly thoughts
Bring about destruction.

Forugh Farrokhzâd
(1933—1967)

IN THE COLD STREETS OF NIGHT

I have no regrets;
Submission fills my thoughts,
A painful submission;
I kissed the cross of my destiny
  at the top of my Golgothas.

In the cold streets of night
Couples always part in hesitation;
In the cold streets of night
There is no sound but
  "Goodbye, goodbye!"

I have no regrets;
It seems as if my heart
  is flowing somewhere beyond time;
Life will repeat my heart
And the blowballs that sail away
  on the lake of the wind
Will repeat me.

Ah! Do you see
How my skin is bursting?
How milk is forming
In the blue veins of my breasts?
How blood is beginning
  its cartilaginous growth
In my patient loins?

I am you,
  you,
And also one who loves,
One who suddenly finds in herself
An obscure tie with thousands

of nostalgic, unclear things;
And I am the strong lust of the earth
That draws in all the waters
To fertilize all the plains.

Listen to my distant voice
In the heavy mist of the dawn incantations;
And look at me in the silence
        of the mirrors
And see how I touch again
The dark depths of all dreams
With the remnants of my hands,
And tattoo my heart like a blood stain
On the innocent moments
        of happiness in life.

I have no regrets;
Talk to me, my beloved,
About the other "I"
Whom you will find
        in the cold streets of night
With the same loving eyes,
And remember me
        in the sad kisses she puts
On the kindly lines
        beneath your eyes.

RED ROSE

Red rose,
Red rose,
Red rose:
He took me to the rose garden,
And in darkness, he threaded
        a red rose in my ruffled hair,
And made love with me
On a red rose petal.

O paralysed pigeons,
O naive, infertile trees,

O blind windows,
Below my heart and deep inside my loins
A red rose has begun to grow,
A red rose,
Red as the flags of revolution.

Ah! I am pregnant, pregnant,
I am pregnant!

BORN AGAIN

All my existence is a dark verse
Which repeats you in itself
And will take you to the dawn
        of eternal growing,
        eternal blossoming.
I breathed you out like a sigh, ah ...
I joined you, in this verse,
To trees, to water, to fire.

Perhaps life is a long street
Where a woman, with a basket in her hand,
passes every day;
Perhaps life is a rope
        with which a man hangs himself
        from a branch;
Perhaps life is a child who returns
        from the school;
Perhaps life is lighting a cigarette
        in the languor
        between two love-makings;
Or the bewildered eyes of a passer-by
Who takes off his hat
And with a meaningless smile
        says "Good morning"
        to another passer-by.

Perhaps life is the closed moment
When my glance melts

in the pupils of your eyes,
And there is a feeling in this
Which I will mingle with my perception
        of the moon and darkness
In a room the size of loneliness;
My heart,
The size of love,
Thinks of the trivial motives
        for its happiness;
Of the beautiful withering
        of the flowers in the vase;
Of the sapling you planted
        in our garden;
And of the singing of canaries
Whose songs are
        the size of a window.

Ah ...
This is my share,
This is my share ...
My share is a sky
That can be taken away from me
        by just drawing the curtain;
My share is descending
        a deserted stairway
To join something in decay
        and alienation;
My share is a sad walk
        in the garden of memories
And dying with the sorrow of a voice
        which says to me:
"I love your hands."

I plant my hands in the garden;
I will grow, I am sure I will grow
And swallows will lay their eggs
In the hollow of my ink-stained hands.

I will hang on my ears
Twin red cherries as earrings,
And I will stick dahlia petals
        on my fingernails;
There is an alley

Where the boys who loved me,
With the very dishevelled hair,
        scrawny necks and thin legs,
Still think of the innocent smiles
        of the little girl
Whom one night the wind
        will take away.

There is an alley which my heart
Has stolen from the surroundings
        of my childhood.

The journey of a mass
        along the line of time;
And with a mass making the barren line
        of time pregnant,
The mass of a conscious image
Returning from the feast of a mirror.

And this is how
Someone dies
And someone else stays alive.
No diver can ever fish pearls
In a narrow stream
        which finishes in a swamp.

I know a sad little fairy
Who lives in an ocean
And plays her heart away bit by bit
        on a flute;
A little, sad fairy
Who dies at night with a kiss
And with a kiss is born again at dawn.

SOMEONE WHO IS NOT LIKE ANYONE ELSE

I dreamed someone is coming,
I dreamed of a red star;
And now
        my eyelids are quivering,
Which is a sign of good omen;

I'm telling the truth;
May God make me blind
      if that's a lie.
When I was not asleep
I dreamed of a red star;
Someone will come,
Someone will come,
Someone different,
Someone better than all the others;
Someone who is not like anybody else;
      not like father, nor like Yah'yâ, [33]
      nor like mother;
He is like what we expect him to be;
And he is much taller than the trees
      in Master Mason's garden,
And his face is brighter than
      the face of the Absent Imam, [34]
And even brighter than the face
      of Sayyed Javâd's brother, [35]
Who became a cop in blue uniform
And he isn't afraid of anyone,
Not even of Sayyed Javâd
      who is our landlord
      and all our rooms
      belong to him.

[33]   *Yah'yâ, the Arabic form of John (the Baptist) is a common name for Iranian men.*

[34]   *Shi' ah Moslems believe in the twelve Imams—Ali and his eleven successors—and call the last one, Mohammad ibn Hassan al-Mahdi, the "Absent Imam", because he is said to have disappeared when five years old. He is believed to be alive and will reappear on the Last Day to spread justice throughout the world by his sword.*

[35]   *Sayyed means "mister" or "lord" in Arabic, but in Iran it is a title for the descendants of the Prophet. Shi' ahs have much respect for these men, who are found in all walks of life. The ironic tone of the passage suggests that the narrator does not expect one Sayyed to be her landlord while another is "a cop in blue uniform".*

Someone will come
Someone whose name,
As mother calls him
    at the beginning
    and at the end of her prayers,
Is the Judge-of-All-Judges,
Or the Satisfier-of-All-Needs;
And he can read
    with closed eyes
All the difficult words
    in the Readers Three;
And he can also subtract a thousand
From twenty million
    without any deficit;
And he can buy on credit
    whatever he wants
    at Sayyed Javâd's shop;
And he can do something
    to the neon sign of Allah
On the dome of the Meftâhiyân Mosque [36]
    to make it shine again
As green as the dawn.

Ah ....
How good is light;
How good is light;
And how I wish Yah'yâ had a pushcart
And a mantle lamp;
And how I wish
I could sit on his pushcart
    among the melons
    and watermelons,
And go round and round Mohammadiyeh Square; [37]

[36]   *Meftâhiyân Mosque is one of the mosques in the south of Tehran, in a poor neighbourhood.*

[37]   *Mohammadiyeh Square is a large square in the poor south of Tehran, also known as "Meydân-e E'dâm" (Execution Square) because until fifty years ago criminals were hanged there.*

Ah ...
How good it is to go
        round and round the square
        on a pushcart;
How good it is to sleep on the roof;
How good it is to walk in a public garden;
How good is the taste of Pepsicola;
How good it is to go to Fardin Cinema; [38]
And how I like all the good things,
And how I wish I could pull the hair
        of Sayyed Javâd's daughter.

Why should I be so small
        that I should be lost
        in the streets!
Why my father, who isn't small
        and doesn't lose his way,
Isn't doing something
        to persuade the one
        whom I saw in my dream,
To bring forward his day of coming;
And why the people who live
        around the slaughterhouse
Aren't doing something?
The people the soil of whose gardens
        is bloodstained,
And so is the water in their fishponds,
And so are the soles of their shoes;
Why don't they do something?
How lazy is the winter sun!
I have swept the stairs to the roof,
And have washed all the windowpanes.

Someone will come,
Someone will come,
Someone who's with us in his heart,
        in his breath, and in his voice.
Someone whose coming can't be arrested,
        handcuffed and put into prison;

[38]   *Fardin was a popular actor in the Shah's time and owned a*
cinema, specialising in the showing of Persian films.

Someone who'll come
        through the rain,
        through the murmur of the rain,
        through the whisper of petunias.
Someone who'll come
        from the sky above Tupkhâneh Square [39]
        in a night of fireworks,
And he will spread the table-cloth
And he will divide the bread,
He will divide the pepsi,
He will divide the public gardens,
He will divide the whooping-cough mixture,
He will divide the school's registration day, [40]
He will divide the hospital tickets,
He will divide the trees of Sayyed Javâd's
        daughter,
He will divide all the rejected goods,
And will also give us our shares
        of everything.

I've had a dream ...

I WILL GREET THE SUN AGAIN

I will greet the sun again;
I will greet the streams which flowed in me;
I will greet the clouds which were
        my lengthy thoughts;
I will greet the painful growth of poplars
Which pass through the dry seasons;
I will greet the flocks of crows
Which brought me, as presents,

[39]   *Tupkhâneh Square, known as Sepah (Army) Square in the Shah's time, was until fifty years ago the largest and most famous square in Tehran. The name means "gun depot" because at one time there was an underground armoury on one side of the square.*

[40]   *Several days before the beginning of the school year on 21 September, parents have to take their children to school to be registered.*

The sweet smells of the fields at night;
I will greet my mother who lived in the mirror
And was the image of my old age;
And I will also greet the earth whose burning womb
Is filled with green seeds by the passion she has
        for reproducing me.

I will come, I will come,
I will come with my hair,
As the continuation of the smells of the soil;
With my eyes, as the dense experiences of darkness,
Carrying the bushes I have picked in the woodlands
        beyond the wall.
I will come, I will come,
I will come and the entrance will be filled with love;
        And at the entrance I will greet again
        those who are in love,
And also the girl who is still standing
At the entrance in diffusion of love.

THE CONQUEST OF THE GARDEN

The crow which flew past above us
And disappeared into the confused mind
        of a wandering cloud
And its cry pierced through the sky
        like a short spear,
Will take our news to the town.

Everyone knows,
Everyone knows that you and I
Saw the garden
Through that cold, gloomy hole,
And picked the apple
From that playful branch
        which was out of reach.

Everyone is afraid,
Everyone is afraid, but you and I
Joined the lamp, the water, and the mirror,

And were not afraid.

It is not the question of the fragile tie
        of two names,
And having intercourse in the old pages
        of a registry book;
I am speaking of my lucky tresses
And the glowing red anemones of your kisses,
And of sincerity of our bodies in stealing,
And of the glittering of our skins
Like the scales of the fish in water;
I am speaking of the silvery life of a song
Which is sung at dawn by a small fountain.

One night, in that flowing green forest
We asked the wild rabbits;
And in that disturbed yet relaxed sea
We asked the oyster laden with pearls;
And also in the remote, triumphant mountain
We asked the young eagles:
"What is to be done?"

Everyone knows,
Everyone knows that we have reached
        the cold and silent sleep of Simorghs; [41]
We have found the truth in the flowerbed,
In the shy glances of an unknown flower;
And we have attained the eternal life
        in the infinite moment
When two suns stared at each other.

It is not the question
        of a frightened whisper in the dark;
I am speaking of daylight
        and open windows;

[41]   *A legendary bird, said to have the plumage found in every bird in
the world, living in the Qâf Mountain.   In Ferdowsi's "Shânnâmeh"
(Book of Kings), the Simorgh brings up the abandoned child, Zâl, who
later becomes the father of Rostam, the greatest hero of Iranian legend.*

Of fresh air and a fireplace
  where all the useless things are burned;
And of a land cultivated with a new crop;
And of birth, perfection and pride;
I am speaking of our loving hands
Which have made a bridge with the messages
  of fragrance, light and breeze
Above the gulf of nights.

Come to the meadow,
Come to the vast meadow
And call me from behind the breaths
  of the silk-tasselled acacia,
Like a gazelle calling its mate.

The curtains are full of a suppressed sob,
And the innocent doves
Are looking at the earth
From the top of their white tower.

Mahmud Kiânush
(b. 1934)

CUCKOO

It was a mid-spring dawn in Nishâbur, [42]
Or was it a mid-winter sunset?
And the willow trees were dancing
        in a gentle breeze,
Or were they dead still
In the solemn silence of a heavy snow?
And Omar Khayyam,
When searching for a striking rhyme
To suit the last line
        of an unfinished Rubâ'i,
Or perhaps still trying to select
From amongst the parading images
The best few for his theme,
Suddenly heard a cuckoo calling him
From the ruins of Persepolis,
Asking in mournful notes:

"Where ... where ... where ...
Where is that might,
That glory of the past,
For the pride of which
The king of kings
Felt free to talk to God
More as a rival than a friend?"

Some thousand years later,
Somewhere in the godless,

[42]   *Nishâbur, a town in the province of Khorâsân, in north-east Iran,
which was the birthplace of Omar Khayyam, the mathematician, as-
tronomer and poet. He is best known in the West for his "Rubâ' iyât"
(meaning Quatrains) rendered into English by Edward Fitzgerald in
1859.*

kingless empire
        of Machine,
Where hope is sterile,
And lies are divine,
I,
One of Omar Khayyam's last true sons,
In the desert of my solitude,
In the ruins of my soul,
Am asking the cuckoo of the clock:

"When ... when ... when ...
When will Man stop drinking
        the hemlock of the Past
To the triumphant reign of the Future,
While in the Present
He lets love die unlived?"

And the wooden bird,
Chained to the wheel of time, replies
In notes alien to the rhythm of my heart:

"Never ... never ... never! "

WITH YOUR ROOTS

With your roots
Deep down in the enchanted soil
        of the Mother's womb;
With your trunk
Rising upright
Through the flying air
        of the Father's mind;
And with your branches,
Though twisted, entangled, cramped
Inside a tiny globe of bone,
Yet grown beyond the reach
        of the wandering stars,
You are a Tree.

Let your fragrant Springs blossom
In the smiles of your lonely eyes
And make my still dawn throb
With the hope of another miracle
        of rain;
Let your ripened Summers fall
In the apples of your glowing words
And awaken my despairing hunger
For the taste of another resurrection
        of Truth.

Hate is only a cold breath of those
For whom Death exists
And means eternal curse:

Do not tremble like a white fuchsia
In the Autumn wind;
War is only a dying spark
From the idle, clapping hands
Of those who have never sipped
The divine wine of Life!

Do not lament the Future
Like a delirious epileptic
In an apocalyptic Winter.
Look at your glorious image
In the mirror of infinity;
The sun is holding a candle.
Do not wait until dawn;
You may forget your dream
When you wake in the Eternal Morning.

A WHITE PIGEON

Man was standing
On the roof of his ivory tower,
Looking at the floating, white clouds
        for inspiration.
He was not sure if all he had done
        on earth

Since the beginning of time
Could ensure his immortality;
And he was reviving his imagination
With wonderful memories,
Making a new plan
In the light of which
       he might see himself
Shaking hands with God
In the pleasure garden of eternal fun.

A white pigeon,
Flying on its way to the nearest pond,
Dropped a piece of its unwanted thoughts.

Man wiped his forehead
With the back of his idle hand
And, in anger and frustration,
Looked up again at the floating,
       white clouds
Wondering on which to put the blame:
The white pigeon,
The white clouds,
Or on the height of his ivory tower!

GEOGRAPHY

The Earth,
My place of exile,
Is bounded on the north by Motion,
On the south by Blood,
On the east by Passion,
And on the west by Repetition.

Its flag Rainbow,
Its coin the Sun,
Its religion Beingness,
Its government Change,
Its industrial products Ashes,
And its spokesman Love.

Its greatest musician the Wind,
Its greatest artist the Spring,
Its greatest poet the Night,
Its greatest philosopher Water,
And its greatest champion Earthquake.

To remain hungry at its generous table
Is a rewardless suffering,
And to eat with greed
Is a sin without punishment.

In its fields
From the ashes of the killed and the killers
Grow grains with the same taste,
And Chastity and Debauchery
Take their ablution under its rains
In the naked body of one blossom.

O Thought,
In this exile
Do not complain about the Beginning.

GLIMPSES

1

It is not your eyes
That show me the way,
But a sudden note
From your heart.

2

Only when I touch your hand
Will all the words burst
Like colourful bubbles
In the breeze of your eyes.

3

Laughing, you left my eyes
In search of the sun,
In the dead sea of a mirror;
The sky will never dawn.

4

When you escape loneliness,
Love is glimmering just ahead;
But it is always hate
            that embraces you
Before you can say who you are.

5

My journey from the Cave
To the emptiness of the Moon
Has been a long agony;
Let me rest a while
Before I set off for Hell.

6

Every spring the Earth
Throws up all the secrets
            entrusted to her;
But I shall break mine to the last one
Before I return to her womb.

7

Only when I walk
By the trees in the sunshine
And hear the call of a bird,
Do I know that life
Is still young and hopeful.

8

Afraid of the deadly snow,
The little bird flew down

To take shelter in the rose bush
Only to burn in a big fire.

9

The universe with all her galaxies
Cannot fill my eyes;
Adorn her with a green leaf,
Then my heart becomes
    a green universe.

10

God created the Earth
And left it idle in the void;
I looked at it with love:
Its beauty shone
And I called it World.

11

Before you fall down
Look around
Into the eyes of those
    who are near you,
And tell them you were also there;
Your voice will not be forgotten.

12

He smiled in his agony
And pointing to the earth,
He whispered to his grieving son,
"Mothers are in love with their wombs,
And their wombs bear death."

13

A thorn pricked my finger
And in my mouth
The taste of raspberries
Mixed with a salty doubt;
A redbreast flew away.

OUTSIDER

I

Can once again
The song of a bird
Make man stop for a few moments
By the shrine of a tree
On his way to destroy life?

II

All my life I have been brooding
Over a single pebble of doubt,
And yet I cannot expect
The lark of a clear thought
        to be hatched,
Because whenever I swallow
One of many fears of the future,
Deep down in my heart I hear
The hissing of a serpent
That tries to break its way
Out of the shell of doubt
Towards the tomorrow of mankind.

III

Whenever I think about Beginning
        of any kind,
Before me I see a circle.
I make my eyes run
Round and round along the fatal line
Until I feel I am nothing but a point
Somewhere on the circle before me,
And in my silent despair I cry:
"Let this be the Beginning!"

I stare at the point on the fatal line,
        And it tells me,
        perhaps with sarcasm:
"Let it be also the End!"

IV

The man you hate
Because he is very stupid,
Is loved by his neighbour
Because he is very kind.
Dead twigs usually make
      the best nests
For beautiful birds
      you usually admire
Their plumage and songs.

V

I say "Hello!"
And they ask my name.
The fish live nameless in the sea,
And they all greet each other.

Without a name I do not exist,
And with a name
I am easily forgotten.

VI

I hide myself
In the bushes of words,
And you seek for me;
Both of us are lost.

Touraj Rahnamâ
(b. 1937)

I AND FREUD

I do not know what is burrowing
So restlessly, so swiftly,
Like a searching mole,
Deep down in my being,
That is a desert of silence.

But sometimes
I hear a voice from the depths
Of this desert of magic and mystery;
A familiar message
With which my withered autumn
Bursts into blossoms.

SKETCH

I thought now it was the time
        to kill the canaries
And scatter their feathers
Upon the Elburz Mountains.

I thought now it was the time
        to tell the Earth,
"Shed the blood of the Sun
With a sharp dagger!"

I thought now it was the time
        to strangle the Moon
By mighty hands
And scatter its feathers
Upon the Elburz Mountains
At the first smile of the Dawn.

Shâdâb Vajdi
(b. 1937)

WAIT FOR ME

And I become alive again
Outside the confines of my body,
Beyond the misery of want,
Among the fruit-laden branches
Within a moment,
Itself begotten by the sun;
And in the shelter of a bush
That carried the pure fragrance
      of love
To the boundless plains;
And my eyes,
Not a pair of mute spheres,
But flames of quest;
And my hands,
Two guiding sails
Speeding towards the green land
      of lovers;
And my soul, my heart
Singing,
      singing.

Wait for me
Along the blue line of the horizon
That leads the silver path
      of the moon
To the glittering fountains
      of stars,
And by the waterfalls of dawn
At the moment when the sun rises
And draws the threads of light
From one branch to another,
Carrying them like grains
Deep inside the nests
Where the chicks,
With desire for light and sky,
Are cheeping,
      cheeping.

Wait for me
At the bright end of my voice
That from above the mysteries
        of the galaxies
Flows down to the earth
To be absorbed by the buds of growth
And to give the slumberers
        of the gardens
Tidings of sunshine and life.

Wait for me;
I will become alive again.

THE MANTLE OF LOVERS

Waiting for you
In every step,
In every breath,
In every glance that slides lovingly
Into the cold maelstrom of memories;
Waiting for you on the summit of a frozen night,
And in the clarity of a day
That sings itself in the nest of light.

How slowly pass
The sounds of seconds
Round the axis of the dungeon of loneliness.
Behold!
It is I,
        passing through the deluge of tears,
Cloaked with the night,
Treading on thorns and rubble;
It is I,
        the old wound of the Earth,
A disturbed dream in the tired mind of the soil.
Where the voice softly fades out
There is a bridge spanned
        to the mystery of the green breaths
        of wakefulness;
It is I,
        having no desire to go or return;
Waiting for you in every moment,
I am sitting with the night
In the mantle of lovers.

Meymanat Mirsâdeghi [Âzâdeh]
(b. 1937)

THE PICTURE OF A BRIGHT WINDOW

I went to the window and said:
"Oh! What glorious sunshine !
What a bright day!
What rich blossoming happiness
Is present in everything!"

I said to myself:
"I will grow with plants,
I will sing with birds,
I will flow with waters."
I said to myself:
"I will drink the day,
— This gold-rimmed goblet
        brimful with sunshine —
In one draught!"

I stayed by the window,
I stayed,
And then my small room
        began to fill with melancholy,
— Heavy black smoke —
 And my desire to grow,
        to sing,
                to flow
Was the picture of a bright window
In this closed space,
Inside these four walls.

The leaden sky of the dusk
With its melancholy, mourning rain
Was softly crying.

Tâhereh Saffârzâdeh
(b. 1938)

RESIGNATION

I walk in town
An aimless walk in town
An endless walk in imagination
Before 4 o'clock p.m.
After 8 o'clock a.m.
Time is mine
I have time to pick up pebbles
     for lazy hands
And wake the moon
Which has been asleep
     on the second page
     of my geography book
     for many, many years
Our poor teacher thought
That it was oceans and mountains
     that divided people.

In the long corridors
     my colleagues meet
     while marking time
I have shared with them
     the closed windows
     and a temperature of 70 to 75 degrees
My colleagues meet and make judgements:
How can she live from now on
Without annual leave
Without her 10 a.m. cup of coffee
Without a boss
I am returning to the seasons of the year
They are still the same old four seasons
The grass still feeds on its chlorophyll
The wind is full of flying spears
The irises are shaking like The Beatles

Yesterday I had promised my headache
       to give it two aspirins
I have still time
Tomorrow afternoon is also mine
I am overflowing with stately pauses
I who hate rough behaviour of bullets.

INVITE ME FOR A SANDWICH OF LOVE

Invite me for a sandwich of love
I'm tired of big lunches
Of big preparations
Of big promises
Don't forget that I'm not the woman
       in Somerset Maugham's *Luncheon* [43]
I'm a traveller
Who has experienced the burden
       of too heavy luggage
Who only thinks
Of light rucksacks
Of light stomachs
Of light memories
Invite me for a sandwich of love
Serve me with your own hands
Wrap me with the paper of your breaths
At the table of this cold winter night.

[43]   *A reference to the woman in Somerset Maugham's short story
"The Luncheon" , who has a strange lust for delicious, costly food.*

Esmâ'il Kho'i
(b. 1938)

TO BE (II)

Like God
I am a self-worshipper:
He puts His marks of existence
        on everything
Lest someone should think
        that the Eternally Hidden One
        does not exist;
As for me, I write
To make it publicly known
        that I exist.

TO BE (IV)

Night like loneliness
Overflowing and profound.
Sorrow like a mountain,
And happiness like its crest,
A crown of snow.
And the sky,
        with its stars
Open like possibility,
Illimitable in all directions.

I, like myself,
        like blossoming,
Or like, I know not what, in springtime;
Perhaps like a forest:
Old and young,
        repetitious and novel.

And I silently ask the stars:
Will this year be like my other years,

One step further towards lostness
Into the void of the memory of nothingness?
Or this time,
      with these buds
Which I see on every branch,
Will it add something
To this timelessly untamable world?

And the luminaries of the sky,
Silent and full of smiles,
Seem to have seen a wakeful forest
Whose old nerves,
      branch by branch,
Are being adorned by the vigour of youthfulness.

WHEN I WAS A CHILD

When I was a child
The flight of a kite
Could take me from the roofs
      of my early-rising eyelids
To the orange groves of the sun.
Ah,
How short were the distances!

When I was a child
Goodness was a woman
Who smelled of cigarettes,
And her large teardrops
Mixed with the chant
      of reading the Koran
Through her spectacles.
And at nights
Crickets chirped
With the music of the moon
      and profound silence.

When I was a child
Pleasure was a line
From a flying stone

To the whining of a sickly old dog.
Ah,
How ruthless were
      those innocent hands!

When I was a child
I could watch the feathers
      of a helpless turtledove
As the wind carried them away
      from the scissor blades;
Yes, I could watch them
And smile with pleasure,
Feeling some pride as cruel
      as sincerity.

When I was a child
One tale was enough
To fill my dreamy days
      and nights of dreams
With joy and excitement
For a Thousand and One Nights.

When I was a child
God was much stronger.

When I was a child
The tamest starlings of delight
Made their nests
On the window-sills of smiles.
Ah,
In those days the cats of Thought
Were not so abundant.
When I was a child
There were no People!

When I was a child
There was sorrow
But
only a little.

THE RICH NORTH ALSO

In our city the poor south
  will be ruined by the rain.

The poor south
  will be ruined
  by the rain;
How strange
  that it cannot touch my heart!

Look!
The cloud has scattered all its sorrow
  into the sphere of rain,
And I,
  who have always been enamoured
  of sorrow,
Stare at the scene,
  but it raises no sad feelings in me.

I look,
And see nothing but the cloud
Which sings its sorrow!
  Is it really so?
  No!
I must celebrate the fall of sorrow
  in the dominion of my soul.

I look,
And see nothing but the cloud
Which cries its nocturnal fury,
And strikes the wild notes
  of its wakeful whip
In the lightning,
  and in my veins.

Tonight I must celebrate
  the decline of all my refined sentiments.
At this moment
I am loud and exploding

like anger,
And like anger
        I am strong;
And I can take the Diwan of Hâfez
And tear it leaf by leaf
        with my own hands; [44]
And, like daggers and like decay,
I can accept
        the necessity of bloodshed
        and of yellowed leaves;
And I can stand up
        at the passage of the wind
And shatter the dew-pearled blossoms
        of all gardens petal by petal;
And I can even watch
        the slaughtering of a thousand
        new born lambs,
        their throats being cut one by one;
At this moment
I am loud and exploding.

In my city the poor south will be ruined,
And there is no reason for regret!

I have faith in clouds;
Surely they know what they do;
It is not in vain
        when they scatter their abundant seeds
Upon this desert of humanity.

In my city the poor south will be ruined
And there is no reason for regret;
There is no reason for regret:
The poor south is doomed to be ruined.

---

[44]   *Tearing the Diwan (Divân) of Hâfez would be considered sacrilege by any Iranian. The Diwan (or collection of ghazals) by Shams-sod-
Din Mohammad Hâfez of Shirâz (1300—1388) is the consummation of
lyrical poetry in Persia.*

"Injustice?
              no, this is not injustice.
To have pity on the lowlands
              is injustice;
To have pity on the bushes of the valleys
              is injustice;
To be on the summits of the mountains
              and have pity on the valleys,
This is what has been injustice
              in all times!" the flood says.
And I also say:
"This has been injustice in all times."

And the flood says:
"All the depths must be filled;
No mountains, no valleys must exist;
All the face of the earth must be levelled;
How beautiful is the smile of the sun
              at the vastness of plains!"

Look!
Here rolls the most magnanimous deluge;
Here roars the powerful, ruthless anger;
Here stampedes a forest
              of mad elephants;
And the horror of devastation
Is tearing time and space asunder!

Look!
The most glorious flood,
Is chanting, with an epic fervour,
As if in praise of the nature's agreement
              with history.
Look!
How well it knows,
And how capable it is!

Look, look!
Who has said
              that destruction is not spectacular?
Who has said
              that destruction is tragic?

184

In our city the poor south
     will be ruined,
And there is no reason for regret:
The poor south will be ruined by the flood,
And the rich north also
     by the ruination of the south.

ON THE ROAD

What I see
Is the permanence of the ocean;
The birth of the garden
     after every winter,
The emergence of days
     out of nights,
And not the transience of waves,
     flowers
          and dewdrops.
Though we pass away,
The road remains;
Therefore, no laments!

GHAZAL-VAREH [V] [45]

> *At the beginning the light of your beauty*
> *opened the door of manifestation;*
> *Love appeared and set fire to the whole*
> *universe. "*
>   *(Hâfez of Shirâz)*

Tonight I feel the resonance of a song in me;
Tonight my heart is illuminated
     with a shower of stars.

[45]   *"Ghazal-vâr" means "like a ghazal" but Esmâ' il Kho' i has added*
another suffix "-eh" to show that he is using a new, or modern, form of
the ghazal without any predesigned metre or rhymes.

Call the words,
Call the words and tell them
        to come to me
With their empty pitchers,
        because tonight
I have in me
        what the rain has in its tambourine,
        what the springs have in their flutes.

Love has revealed itself.
The silk of its breaths
Stroked my face in the wind.
Its fragrance could be felt
        in the morning tenderness.
Love has revealed itself,
        I am sure;
Love has appeared again.
O my heart!
You cold, desolate ash!
Drink the breaths of flames,
        drink them.

I bring you good news, dear Autumn;
The migrant swallows have returned;
Again in the plains of cold ashes
The cups of tulips are in flames.

I bring you good news, dear Night;
Light has taken wing
And *'the whole universe is aglow'*. [46]

I bring you good news, O delicate Silence,
O rich Poetry,
Tonight there is a song in me,
My heart has become a heart again.

[46]   *A reference to the image in the verse from Hâfez, which Kho'i uses as the epigraph to this poem. It is an image which has been used by many Persian mystic poets.*

This reunion is a new beginning,
It is the light of your beauty,
And manifestation
        and ascension with joy.

But now it is better for me
        not to breathe a word.

GHAZAL-VAREH [XXIII]

She is beautiful like understanding,
        like solitude,
And necessary like certainty,
        like beauty
And like love she is necessary
        and beautiful;
My beloved is a star of rain
On the face of dawn.

In the clarity of her mirror,
My beloved is the green-clad goddess
        of Springs,
Walking softly on the bridge
        of rainbow,
With her hair of water,
Her arms of sunshine,
Her bosom of pure rapture,
And with glances whose horizons
        spread beyond the beyond,
She takes me to a realm
        where I can attain
        the joy of poetry
        and the peace of nothingness.

My beloved is pure rapture;
She is of water,
        she is of sunshine.

When I look at her
        with my inner eyes,
Suddenly the world seems beautiful,
And I realize how blind,
        how ignorant, I have been!

When I look at her
        with my inner eyes,
Suddenly ugliness, falsehood and evil
        cease to exist;
And I see that my poetry is brimmed
        with water, sunshine and rapture,
And the peace of my nothingness
        with whatever is good,
        with whatever is beautiful,
        and whatever is true.

When I look at her
        with my inner eyes,
Suddenly I feel that God exists
And whatever exists is necessary
        and beautiful,
And I realize how ignorant,
        and how blind I have been.

Ah ...
From the rapture of poetry
To the peace of nothingness
All is my beloved.

WITH IMMENSE SMALLNESS

The small fish of this stream
Will never bear whales.
I am well aware of my immense smallness,
And accept it with resignation.

But when the falling of a pebble,
        like a powerful hand,

Breaks the one-thousand-year sleep
      of a swamp,
It is not in vain, no doubt,
That the fist of anger
Pounds against the wall of my heart.

BREAKFAST IN EXILE

I wake up.

Outside
Shines the sun,
But not on the shoulders
      of Elburz Mountains.

On the table
      the empty place of a cup;
Beside it
The cold cup of loneliness
Brimful
With black coffee of sorrow.

Mansur Owji
(b. 1939)

ONE NIGHT, WHEN ...

One night,
One night, when all the lovers
      are asleep,
Let your selfhood fall down
      at your feet
Like a ripened fruit.

Forests cultivate their trees
With continuous decay,
With continuous growth;
And new roots meet each other
Down in the soil;
Holding each other's hands,
The lovers grow side by side
      under the sun.

TWICE A YEAR

He had bought it
      from some vendor
In one of the streets of Shirâz;
An old picture in an old frame:
A woman, a stranger
With a shawl of dust
      covering her head
And her fingers playing
      on a fiddle ...

Since then,
Twice a year , the house fills
      with music,
With the exuberance of children
      dancing.

Ne'mat Mirzâzâdeh [M.Âzarm]
(b. 1939)

MEMORY

Suddenly at midnight
      heavy snow began to fall
like a new-blown memory.
It seemed I had seen her once before
      in a time like this,
      under such a wondrous snow.
When, with strong desire, I opened my mouth
      to read my new-found memory aloud,
And, looking into her eyes,
      asked the sky of my faraway homeland
      about the stars,
My voice melted on my lips like snowflakes,
And her face suddenly blossomed
From the dawn of a memory.

Mohammad Rezâ Shafi'i Kadkani [M. Sereshk] (b. 1939)

IN THE NAME OF THE RED ROSE

Sing in the name of the Red Rose
In the deserts of the night,
So that all the gardens
      may awake and bloom.
Sing, sing again,
      so that the white doves
May return to their blood-covered nests.

Sing in the name of the Red Rose,
In the hall of silence,
So loud that the echo of your voice
May pass through the plains;
Sing the shining message of the rain
On the blue dome of the night;
So that the passing breeze
May take it to all the horizons.

What is that fear of drought in you?
Many a dam they erected
Not against water,
      but against light,
Against songs and joys ...

In this time of hardship
They have given permits to the poets
For writing poems deeper than sleep
And clearer than water
About the love affairs
Of cedars, turtle-doves and tulips.

If you remain silent,
      who do **you expect** to sing?
If you go away,
      who do you expect to stay?
Who will sing for our leafless young tree?

Look beyond this pass,
There, in that other land
The spring,
          having passed through barbed wires,
Has gloriously arrived.
See how beautiful is
          the sulphurous fire of the violets!

A thousand mirrors are in flow,
A thousand mirrors are throbbing with delight
In harmony with your heart.
The earth is left empty of carousing lovers;
Now it is you alone who can sing again
The most passionate love songs.
Sing in the name of the Red Rose;
'Tell the story of love
In that secret language you know!' [47]

TO WATER

I

At night the river
With the words it had learned
From the clouds and valleys,
Composed its pastoral, fluent song of water
In praise of the flowers of your blush;
And now
Every small stream I see flowing by
Repeats that melodious song of love.

II

The fluent poem of the stream
Has become so much a part of me
That it softly repeats itself in my ears,
Like the memory of sweet folksongs of Khorasan,
In the streets of my childhood.

[47]   *A quotation from one of the ghazals of Hâfez.*

It is so delicate,
        so profound and sincere
That I wonder who has really composed
This ecstatic song of love,
I or the rain?

III

Like the tree of Zoroaster's miracle,
Like the Cedar of Kâshmar, [(48)]
With shining green foliage of springtime,
I rise towards the light of dawn
From the shade of riverbanks.

At this moment
I am no longer what I was;
In my inner self
I am singing of the sea
        and the morning sun,
And will sing
As long as the river of your melodious words
So cheerfully flows by.

IV

O rain!
Tonight the clarity of your poetry
Has become the mirror
        of my imagination and imagery,
With such an influence
That now,
        in the presence of love
And the spirit of songs,
To you I dedicate
All my poetical works.

[(48)]   *In Ferdowsi' s "Shâhnâmeh" (Book of Kings) King Goshtâsb, who
has been directed in the path of wisdom by Zoroaster, plants a cedar tree
outside one of the many fire-temples he has erected. The cedar was a
gift sent by God from paradise.*

Mohammad-Ali Sepânlu
(b. 1940)

from THE PAVEMENTS

O the tormented world,
Smiling at your empty bowl
    with etiquette,
The pavements remember;
After the gunfire of curfew
— The continuance of a sunset
    in massacre —
Devastated by security and order,
The pavements remember;
They are, like oblivion,
    brimful with a lost intellect.

The washed, naked shores
After a tempest ...
The spatter of blood
    on the windowpanes
    of the horizon;
The appearance of a rainbow bridge,
And on the bridge
    the birds are expecting
    a rainstorm.

A high mist is hovering
    over the village
And a frightening smoke
    above the factories;
The sound of measuring
    and verifying
    the length of the moments,
The sound of drums
    rolling in the space ...

Inside the sombre cafes
      full of damp and smoke,
We drink tea
And the radio reports
      of a revolution
In a distant sky,
      after a barrage of gunfires.

A breeze blows out of the radio
And makes one's hair stand on end;
What cold days!
What blossoming seasons are waiting
      in the shelter of Spring!

Spring, the high dome of young
      aspirations.

Ahmad-Rezâ Ahmadi
(b. 1940)

POEM NINE: FOR SPRING

I will reveal my heart to you
       only when clothes
       would no longer be black
And you would bury
       the mourning day of gazelles
       and lovers
In the calendar
In the springtime of my house.

Because the earth is small
And I was born on the earth
My home is on the earth.

Look,
In the corner of my room
       again in your absence
       rain is falling.

In the corner of my room
The blood in your veins suspects
       that I am going to die
But beside my old hands
       blossoms employ the clouds as ladders
       to reach the summit
       of the spring.

The red blossom has grown
       not from your blood
       but from my youth
I who always know
I who have hunger for your hearts.

Who knows for sure that it is cloudy
Who knows that I know

the name of the day
When rain fell only in the street
When the man in the street
          called the knife and died
And the breaths of the man
          still bore the sound of trees
The trees alongside which
          I walked home in my childhood
And the cloud in our house
          dauntlessly embroidered
          on the mourning costumes
          the name of the man
Which was also the name of the sea
          the name of the wound.

At the growth of sadness
I gave the name of the man
          to your voice
Your voice is good
Do call my name.

Now the rain only falls on the knife
Call me to separate the knife
          from the rain
Now the knife is warmer than
          the harbour
The knife is blunt
The knife is dark.

Your voice is good
In your voice the young boats grow
They mature
And become ships.

The warmth of the harbour
          is more than that of the knife's
The ship arrives at the harbour
The warmth of the knife
          becomes cargo for the ship
The ship leaves the harbour
It reaches your voice
And it is because of your silence

That the ship melts
  and turns into a boat.

We reach home on the boat
A planet of warmth
  comes as a guest into my room
In my room I talk to you
  about my heart
Outside the room clouds are waiting
  for you
You who have no winter clothes with you
I speak of my heart to you
  in my room
But the room is too large for you
You who have small hearts
I speak to planets about my heart.

Your houses are small
You have small hearts
I do not reveal my heart to you
Open the window

My heart is useful for the spring.

Esmâ'il Nuri-Alâ [E.N. Payâm]
(b. 1943)

THEIR EXPECTATION

They cover the coffins of the slain
    with our national flag
So that our respect for the colours
Should not allow us to protest
    against the massacres.
The dead lie in battered boxes,
    in deep silence,
Expecting us to speak for them.

They open their coffins,
Just like rose-water bottles,
And the fragrance of their expectations
    fills our hands.

Unwashed and unshrouded
The bodies of the killed
    are buried
In a field well-ploughed for them
    to be sown.
The dead submit themselves
    to the coolness of the soil
    in serene silence,
But in their submission lies
    an urgent expectation.

Over their graves
    heavy stones are placed;
Wondering we ask ourselves:
"Are these stones signs of respect,
Or only to prevent their resurrection?"

They lie in the earth, solemn and silent
Heedless of the red tulips
    planted on their graves.

Minâ Asadi
(b. 1943)

A RING TO ME IS BONDAGE

I do not think of prayer-mats,
But I do think of a hundred roads
Which pass through a hundred gardens
        full of silk-tassel trees;
I know the Kibla; [49]
It has its place where happiness is;
And I say daily prayers
On the Silk Roads,
With the music of sparrows.

I do not know what Affection means,
Or what can be the difference
        between one land and the other.
Aloneness is what I call Happiness
And desert is what I call Home,
And whatever makes me sad I call Love.

To me a five-pound note means Wealth;
I describe anyone who picks a flower
        as Blind;
And in my eyes a net,
        that separates the fish from water,
        is Murderer.

I look at the sea with envy
And say to myself:
"How small you are!"
Perhaps the sea

[49]   *The Kibla (or Ghebleh) is the direction towards which Moslems face when they say their five daily prayers. It is, of course, towards the Ka'bah or House of Allah in Mecca.*

Also feels the same
When it joins the ocean!

I do not know what is Night,
But Day is what I understand well.
To me a flower-bush is a Village
And a short walk in the gardens
        of memories, Freedom,
And any meaningless smile, Joy.
To me anybody who has a cage
        in his possession
        is a Gaoler;

And I see any thought
        that may remain useless in my mind,
        as a Wall;
To me a ring is Bondage.

I do not think of prayer-mats,
But I do think of a hundred roads
Which pass through a hundred gardens
        full of silk-tassel trees.

Zhilâ Mosâ'ed
(b. 1948)

FLIGHT

Sickly walls,
Drained of colour,
Drained of blood,
Stand firmly on their feet.
Gently I touch
The shining blue of the curtain
And like me everything takes
        a fresh breath
In the Kingdom of Heaven;
And the turning circle of light
Wildly takes flight
Out of the empty room.

JUSTICE

The existence
Takes a strange colour;
A small heart begins to beat fast;
The world is frozen down;
A boy shouts out the names
        of his dead fathers;
He holds forward his hand
To be cut from the wrist
        as the penalty of stealing;
A rainbow of cruelty
Covers the heavens;
The boy thinks of his brothers
Who are still dreaming of bread;
        and they have sound hands;
And then he falls down unconscious
By the horrible stroke of justice.

SHAME

Unfamiliar with the blue of the sky,
Unfamiliar with the shining green
      of the earth,
Unfamiliar with the history
      of man's covering his body,
I am standing
Inside a circle of ice,
Surrounded by sorrow and anxiety;
And naked, ancient and alone,
I carry on my shoulders
      the thousand-year-old burden
      of shame,
      of coveredness,
      of modesty.
O mothers of sleep
Whose bones
Are the ancient hiding place
      of the dead instincts,
Look how my bare, ancient roots,
Slowly but with resolution,
Penetrate the ice.

IT IS COLD

It is cold;
Trees are forced to give up
Their garments to the wind,
And the rustling of each leaf
Is another warning
Of the insidious passage of Death.

It is cold;
And only words,
Like a warm rain of stars
Pour into the night of Man.

Ali-Rezâ Nurizâdeh
(b. 1949)

HASSIBA BOULMERKA [(50)]

O my sister in the uprising,
Did you see
How that tormented Algerian girl
Succeeded to avenge you
        on all those men who say,
"Her hair,
(The fragrant mist of ebony
With those bewitching curls)
Gives shelter to little Satans!"
(Who make their false virility tremble!)

In that glorious atmosphere
        of the Olympic Games,
Did you see
How she flew in the air
With wings of championship
        rather than run on the ground,
Without veil, without chaperon,
Fearless of the acid-throwers?

Did you see
How that Algerian sister of yours,
Amid the cries of jubilation,
Stood up as the most beautiful, naked woman
        of history,
Graceful and proud?
It was the power of your sorrows
        burning in her legs,

[(50)]   *An Algerian woman who won an Olympic gold medal in the 1500
metres in 1992.   The fundamentalist Imams in her country called her
"indecent", because she refused to wear the veil and let her naked arms
and legs be seen in public.*

As if she was the embodiment
of your sufferings,
O my sister in the uprising.

She was like a dove
Flying high above those male vultures
Who still sharpen their claws of malice
On the rotten rocks of traditions,
Where female birds
Shower the adorable body
of that victorious woman
With songs of light.

Now the most beautiful fairy of history
Draws with her feet
The image of the dawn of freedom
On the glass of the night.

Mirzâ Âghâ Askari [Mâni]
(b. 1950)

HAPPY IS THE WORLD !

Five smooth ships
  swiftly sail across the ocean of Time;
They resemble five wild horses
  rising from the depths of the dawn.

How wonderful!
The witless ghosts of stone,
On their dark road to death,
  fade away.

I had said to you:
"The painted dead,
With all the ornaments of life
Are still nothing but corpses."

I had said to you:
"The idolaters know only two words,
Idol and Servitude!"

Now the valleys of death
Are devouring those
  who are dead in thought and action,
And the age of silence
Cracks its last whip!

Five mythical ships
Sail on across the ocean of Time;
They resemble five horsemen
  beamed out from the abyss
  of darkness.

Now the age of suffering
Cracks its last whip,

And coffins are taking the idols
On their journey without return.
My sweetheart,
Sing your song,
        the drum beat of our hearts,
At the bedside of the last sleepers,
For the world has no choice
        but a perpetual blooming.

When I was born, my sweetheart,
I heard nothing but bitter tales of sorrow,
And when I became a poet,
I portrayed the deserving
        with joyful images,
But dispersed the undeserving
        with words of bitterness,
For they neither gave out
        the smell of their time,
Nor could enjoy
        the taste of meaning in words.

The age of silence
Cracks its last whip,
And death takes the undeserving
        on their journey without return.
Thanks to the end of decay
        the world becomes new!
And five glorious ships sail in
        on the ocean of Time.
They are five Continents
Embracing each other,
Ready to sing their common song.

Hamid-Rezâ Rahimi
(b. 1950)

A QUARTER TO DESTRUCTION

I live
Like a bird that does not know why it sings;
Like a tree that does not know why it grows;
Like a breeze that does not know why it blows;
And like a fish that does not know
      why all the rivers of the world
      empty in the frying pans ...

Sometimes I think that a flower is something beautiful,
And there is no doubt that it leads me
      to the blessed ancestors of plants.
Sometimes I think that the sky is also beautiful
And this cloud that is about to rain
      is willing to wash away
The ancient sorrow of my heart;
And this wind that has galloped all the way,
      from a faraway land
Down to the throat of my wounded window
Is willing to sweep away my chronic *ennui*.
Sometimes I think that this country is beautiful
And the streets of its towns have familiar traits;
Sometimes I see the image of my childhood
Riding on the waves,
From one river to another,
Or amid the commotion of the street
      idling around
To break a windowpane here,
To draw a matchstick man there
On the tired face of a wall.

Sometimes I see myself
Inside the eyes of a youth
The echo of whose footsteps

Is the favourite music of the girls in love,
And whose breaths have the smell of springs,
      the smell of poetry;
And sometimes I see myself
In the shape of a walking stick
Carrying a handful of sorrows, memories and history
In a small, empty yard.

I see my sister
In a corner
Talking to the mirror;
I see my mother persistently asking the breeze
      about me;
I see my father,
The last days of whose life fade away like smoke
While waiting in the queue for rationed cigarettes;
And the people
Who squeeze their hearts in their hands
Like grenades;
And I see a God
Who has hidden Himself
Behind the face of the moon
For the fear of His people.

Again my wife,
Who finds me drowning
In a cup of cold tea
Rushes to my rescue
Like a brisk lifeguard
And skilfully draws me out.

The time is a quarter to destruction.

BLOCKAGE

Everywhere is closed;
Buildings seem to have
      no doors at all;
Everything seems
      to be withering away,

Even that young tree
        which every morning
Suddenly grew with love
        in my barren mind;
Even that smiling window
Which was always brimming over
        with the music of rain;
Even that china doll
        on whose morning stroll
The clock on the wall
        struck eight.

The city is empty
        of its nightly merriment,
And the stars
        seem to be a handful of pebbles
Scattered on the sky's face
        by an angry man.

Oh, what is the matter with me?
What have I dreamed
        in my frightening wakefulness,
        that today
Everything,
        everybody,
                everywhere,
Seems like a naked wall to me!

INCLINATION

One's throat must be like a garden
And one's eyes like windows
        through which love passes;
And one's stature
Must be like a tree
        which rises out of rocks;
And poetry must be like a singing bird,
Perching on the highest branch of a tree,
Breaking the heavy silence of the world.

Asadollâh Sha'bâni
(b. 1958)

CHILDREN IN FLAMES

Come to welcome me,
Impatient,
With your hair flying in the wind,
A carnation between your lips.
In all the streets
The chariot of the sun
Is passing through the broken windows.
Call me
From behind the hedges of fire,
With hands
Waving through layers of destruction.

Without you
I weep the loneliness of trees
In emptiness.
With helpless eyes
I hold a hand on the Sun's brow.
No voice assures me
Of kindness of Earth;
In the years of stone
I expect you to utter a word
In the time of indifference,
On the passage of the unripe bodies
Of the children in flames
      in the wind.

LIKE A GREEN FINCH

Green
Like the Spring,
I mean the colour of your hands.
I want to be like rain
Falling in drops,
Drip,
      drip,
            drip,
On the music of the Earth.
I want to be a sun,
Or a pomegranate,
Hanging on a branch;
Or a heart,
Pierced by the arrow of love;
I want to be like a green finch
In flight above the town,
Perching,
      here and there,
            on the trees.

Listen to that faraway voice
Coming from beyond the high mountains;
Open all the windows!
In every house I have a lonely heart,
Like a green finch in a cage,
Wistfully calling you.

Behruz Eftekhâri
(b. 1966)

from SYMBOLS

1

Sometimes I fly away
    with the mind of the wind,
    beyond the farthest stars
    and pick up the most attainable
        desires,
    the innermost memories,
        of the clouds,
And put them into the empty baskets
So that when it rains,
The loneliness of the young roses
    of your garden
        should not be revealed.

2

Mountains were the adamant thoughts
    of the Earth;
The rain
Made the adamant thoughts turn into dust
    and run in the rocky bed
    of the river.
Forests were the green desires
    of childhood;
The rain
Made the jaundice of a memory
    run in the narrow mind
    of the river.
Mountains and forests are bridges,
And the Spring approaches
    with graceful steps.

6

Shadows
Are the silent guards of bodies,
Bodies which grow old and disappear;
Shadows are dark-clad Sufis
      of the night,
A night in which
The assault of *ennui* and despair
Breaks one's human stature.
Shadows are the heralds
      of the moments of Death
And their songs distance
      and loneliness.

14

The tears of the fish
Fried in the pan of dawn;
Their aroma smelled
Of the fisherman's blood.

The sun descended the stairs
      of clouds
And the hunger of the fisherman
Shouted the murmurs of fire.

And at night
Every wave was a cry
And with the cries
      the fish's bodies
      wore out more and more;
And it was the expectation
      of another dawn
That disturbed the fisherman's sleep.

My house is a poem
Stained with ink and blood;
Its windowpanes
Smell of roses and stars,
And its gate is where the steps
     of imaginations
      are scored ...

I have seen many houses
     in far distances;
At their gates many birds
     pick up the grains of love
In a rainbowed space.